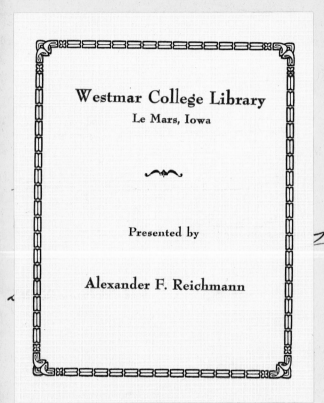

MR. JUSTICE HOLMES

One is almost ashamed to praise a dead master for what he did in a field where he was acknowledged to be supreme. When his work is finished it is too late for praise to give the encouragement which all need, and of which the successful get too little. Still, there is a pleasure in bearing one's testimony even at that late time, and thus in justifying the imagination of posthumous power on which all idealists and men not seeking the immediate rewards of success must live. —*Holmes on Maitland.*

The secret of happiness is freedom, and the secret of freedom is a brave heart.—*Pericles.*

Mr. Justice Holmes

From the portrait by Charles Hopkinson in the Law School of Harvard University

MR. JUSTICE HOLMES

BY
FRANCIS BIDDLE

NEW YORK

CHARLES SCRIBNER'S SONS

1942

Copyright, 1942, by

CHARLES SCRIBNER'S SONS

Copyright, 1942, by Harper & Bros.

Printed in the United States of America

A

Acknowledgments

For permission to quote from books published by them, the author wishes to thank the following: The Central Book Company, for quotation from *Justice Oliver Wendell Holmes: His Book Notices and Uncollected Letters*, by Harry C. Shriver; Coward McCann, for quotation from *Law and the Modern Mind*, by Jerome Frank; Dodd, Mead and Company, for quotation from *Alice James: Her Brothers, Her Journal*, edited by Anna Robeson Burr; E. P. Dutton and Company, for quotation from *New England: Indian Summer*, by Van Wyck Brooks; Harcourt, Brace and Company, for quotation from *Collected Legal Papers of Oliver Wendell Holmes*; Harvard University Press, for quotation from *The Holmes-Pollock Letters*, edited by Mark DeWolf Howe; Houghton Mifflin Company, for quotation from *The Education of Henry Adams*; Little, Brown and Company, for quotation from *Speeches*, by Oliver Wendell Holmes, *The Common Law*, by Oliver Wendell Holmes, *Letters of William James*, edited by Henry James, and *Thought and Character of William James*, by Ralph Barton Perry; The Macmillan Company, for quotation from *Roosevelt: The Story of a Friendship*, by Owen Wister; The Vanguard Press, for quotation from *Justice Oliver Wendell Holmes*, by Silas Bent; Yale University Press, for quotation from *Twilight of the Supreme Court*, by E. S. Corwin.

MR. JUSTICE HOLMES

I

It is too early to determine what Mr. Justice Holmes will mean to future generations of Americans. To some of us who knew him there occurs at times a sense that, like most great men, particularly men who have lived to be very old, he should be rescued from the adulation that has blurred the sharpness of his reality. A reaction might have been expected, but curiously enough it has found expression only in an article or two in some occasional law review, suggesting that when all was said and done Holmes was no more than the flower of a polite culture that missed the cruder complexities of the age of the machine. But his figure, in its vigor and maturity, is not realized, certainly not by the younger generation. Some day the authentic biography will be forthcoming; but before that a briefer word may discover something of the essence of the man.

It would be easy but inadequate to recall him chiefly as a great wit, with an incomparable touch. Things he said had the rare quality of tempered irony. His words were feathered arrows, that carried to the heart of the target, from a mind that searched and saw. Words and thought were so closely knit that the thought could not have been said differently, the words re-arranged. They were warm with his own feeling, incisive with the precision of his mind, or tender, so that they became his words, and others had not used them before. He was a great stylist. Or, perhaps, as the word somehow conveys to our minds the suggestion of polish and surface without the depths below, I should suggest rather the inevitableness of his language. "His conversation and bearing," wrote his friend Morris Cohen, "were like a rare music that lingers in one's memory."

Then there are so many good stories. . .

In a sense he is already an epic memory, the nucleus of a legend. It seldom happens that lawyers whose time converged on his, or even the younger men, coming to thought after his death, can sit together long without the talk moving into what Holmes had said and how he had said it. The extraordinary thing is that the stories have kept their shape, though most have not been put down, and still ring with his quality. The feel of the man has not been lost, the sense of his having lived and talked and written in the grand manner.

Perhaps that very quality, conspicuous as it was in him, has obscured to those who did not know him a deeper understanding of his greatness. The whole picture is too balanced, too rich, too amazingly complete to take in at a glance. Besides, the younger minds are cynical, and youth in shaping its visions is not constrained with the necessity of history, let alone its doubtful importance.

I am not certain whether great judges are inevitably great men. But I have no doubt that Holmes' pre-eminence in the law—Lord Haldane thought that he was second not even to Marshall—was the reflection of his stature as a human being. His maturity in legal thinking was the expression of a maturity in character that occurred early in his growth, and was largely completed when he was mustered out of the Union Army in 1864. Arthur D. Hill has said of him:

Perhaps, however, Justice Holmes's greatest contribution both to his profession and his state and country has been his personality. His name will survive because he has been a great human figure more than by reason of the legal questions in the decision of which he has

3

had a part. The controversies which excite the passions of one generation are often forgotten in the next. The men who dealt with them at once nobly and faithfully remain to inspire succeeding generations . . . Justice Holmes's greatest service as a lawyer was that he showed to all men that the law need not be a dreary competition of sordid interests and that "a man may live greatly in the law as well as elsewhere."

It was an amazing life, hardly annotated for the historian without creative imagination, so placid on the surface, so rich in background of tradition and scope of friends both American and English— Emerson, Henry Adams, William and Henry James, John Chipman Gray, Owen Wister, Felix Frankfurter, Walter Lippmann, Dicey, Maitland, Sir Frederick Pollock, Margot Asquith, Leslie Stephen, Bryce, Haldane, Harold Laski.

If ever a man was to the manner born it was Holmes. But neither this, nor that he was a child of fortune, touched his ultimate simplicity. He was an extraordinarily gallant soldier; before he was forty the author of a book that became famous all over the world, that the London *Spectator* generously (for the London *Spectator*) hailed as "the most original work of legal speculation which has appeared in English since the publication of Sir Henry Maine's *Ancient Law*"; associate justice of the supreme court of his own state the next year and chief justice seven years later; then came the Supreme Court of the United States for the last years; and, as he grew older, as he grew to be a very old man, the nation-wide adoration, although he almost never made speeches or wrote articles or followed causes. They claimed him as theirs, those liberal and progressive forces in American life, about whose opinions he cherished a tolerant skepticism even if a good deal of curiosity. "Probably I am too skeptical," he writes, "as to our ability to do more than shift disagreeable burdens from the shoulders of the stronger to those of the weaker. . . I believe that the wholesale social regeneration which so many now seem to expect, if it can be helped by conscious, co-ordinated human effort, cannot be affected appreciably by tinkering with the institution of property, but only by taking in hand life and trying to build a race. . . The notion that with socialized property we should have women free and a piano for everybody seems to me an empty humbug. . ." And he then adds, with a characteristic ear toward youth: "But it is a pleasure to see more faith and enthusiasm in the young men; and I thought that one of them made a good answer to some of my skeptical talk when he said, 'You would base legislation upon regrets rather than upon hopes.' "

The events for a biographer are but modestly recorded. There are no letters as a boy, none out of the war. There is the history of the Massachusetts Twentieth, not very lively reading, with only a casual reference or two to Holmes, and the bare bones of their battles, and their quarters and the casualties, out of which to create the three years that were forming his will and much of his philosophy. "The 20th never wrote about itself to the newspapers, but for its killed and wounded in battle it stood in the first half-dozen of all the regiments of the north."

After the war his life runs serenely and with little external eventfulness for seventy years, twenty as a student and scholar, fifty as a judge. His personal life was happy and undramatic. His public service was solely on the bench, where the clashes were necessarily intellectual. Our material lies in his writings—the single book, the few articles, the opinions, a steady stream of letters which gradually are coming to the surface, the handful of wonderful speeches. The account must be the story of an extraordinary human being, with little of the external happenings which cluster around most public men.

Even his splendid health is uneventful. It is related to his sound New England self-discipline, behind the shrewd vigor of his mind. He cared passionately for a strong body, not to keep fit for work or for any end—there was but one end, life itself; and life was the getting of all there was out of it, physically, mentally, and in that deeper loneliness of the spirit. "On the whole," he writes Lady Pollock in 1902, "I am on the side of the unregenerate who affirm the worth of life as an end in itself as against the saints who deny it."

Almost the first thing he said to me when in the autumn of 1911 I went to Washington to be his secretary for the next judicial year of the Supreme Court (and he said it to the rest of us) was: "My son, my philosophy is divided into two parts, each equally important: the first—keep your bowels open; and the second—well, the second is somewhat more complex and a part of your duties is to hear it during the next nine months." Part of the duties . . .

I was in Washington the year he died, and, during the days immediately before, I used to stop at 1720 I Street to hear how he was. He was very old, life was far behind him, death waited like a friendly stranger. I rang the bell. How was the Judge tonight? Mary was near tears, but felt they were not fitting.

She shook her head.

"No better?"

"He's a little weaker tonight, sir."

I wanted details, knowing there were none, there could be none.

"I suppose . . . I suppose they let him eat hardly anything."

Her eyes flashed with indignation. "Indeed, and he has his porridge every morning for breakfast."

No, the biographer's problem is not easy. Holmes was extraordinarily human, yet without the weaknesses which make it easier to create the sense of humanity. For his humanity grew from his very strength—the straight body, the strong shoulders, the erect posture, clean skin, long intelligent fingers, his wonderful searching eyes. It was not a strength that seized or dominated or directed—it was a bal-

8

anced power that used the contradictions of his nature and fused them to a single end. He was skeptical of course, yet burned with a passionate faith in life itself. His instincts sought the meaning of life, searched for unity, and for a chance for interstellar generalities. Yet he discarded all explanations as being nothing more than what he called divine gossip. Himself a man of thought, and, doubting that he could play a great rôle as a man of action, he paid tribute to the master builders—Morgan, Hill, Harriman—yet despised the materialism for which he knew they were largely responsible, and loved the romantic in his world because it was gallant rather than successful.

When John D. Rockefeller went to heaven, Holmes told his secretary, he was apprehensive. After all, though he'd been successful and hard working, there were those who had called him a malefactor. . . They let him in the gates. But he had to wait a long time, while others went by, until Saint Peter called him from where the Saint sat behind his desk. "Come here, little man," said the Saint. "I am John D. Rockefeller." "I know," said the Saint, "but you cannot have a front seat. All your life you have been so busy grubbing and add-

ing and toiling and saving that you never knew
what you were doing. You were never conscious of
where you were going. You are entitled only to a
back seat. By my Master's instructions," said Saint
Peter, "the front seats are reserved for those who
were conscious of what they were doing. . ."

Is it any wonder that a legend should gather
round such an extraordinary creature, who happened also to be a great judge? The legend has deep
roots; for, when he died, and now today, when we
are in another war, it is more powerful than ever.

His secretaries have perhaps done much to keep
the Holmes tradition fresh and not inexact. He
grew fond of most of us, I think, and shared his
intimacy of mind and heart with us on the long
rambles that he used to take after the Court work
was over for a brief spell—he was a quick worker
—philosophic interstices, as he thought of them,
between the grind and grind of work which he
hated to think about and loved to conquer. Then he
would immerse himself again with furious concentration. . .

The names of the secretaries and their addresses
appear on the last page of the "black book." The

black book begins with notes on the early reading in 1871—Tissot's *Droit Pénal étudié dans ses principes;* Ortolan, Michelet, Scheurl, Thorpe's *Ancient Laws and Institutes of England*, James Mill's *Jurisprudence*. In 1881 Holmes begins to list the books read each year, sometimes the dates. These cover nearly fifty years; and then at the end the list of secretaries. There were thirty, and I was number seven, between Irving S. Olds, now chairman of the United States Steel Corporation, and Stanley Clarke, trustee of the Associated Gas and Electric Company. Among them were George L. Harrison, president of the New York Life Insurance Company; Harvey Hollister Bundy, special assistant to the present Secretary of War; and, much later, W. Barton Leach, now teaching at the Harvard Law School; Charles Denby, of Pittsburgh; Thomas Corcoran; Donald Hiss, now with the State Department; Mark DeWolfe Howe, Dean of the Buffalo Law School; and, last, James Henry Rowe, Jr., the present Assistant to the Attorney General of the United States.

Horace Gray, who had preceded Holmes on the Supreme Court, had been in the habit of selecting a Harvard Law School graduate to be his law secretary. One of the first, in 1888, had been Samuel Williston, whom later, as a humorous and wise teacher in the Socratic method, so many generations of Harvard Law School men learned to love. John Chipman Gray, a half brother of Justice Gray and a very old friend of Holmes—he also had fought through the Civil War, and it was said that he brought to Lincoln the dispatches announcing the fall of Fort Sumter—was teaching real property at Harvard when Holmes was appointed; and, until 1915, when Gray died, he selected Holmes' secretaries for him from the third year law-school men. After that, Holmes' friend, Professor Felix Frankfurter, chose them. Gray was just the right man to make the selections, for though a great scholar he had no pedantry, but possessed, as Holmes said of him when he died, "the light touch and humor of a man of the world." Gray knew the kind of boys Holmes wanted—they must be able to deal with the *certiorari*, balance his checkbook, and listen to his tall talk. And they would have more chance of understanding it, thought Gray, if they also were honor men. . .

On the flyleaf of the black book there are a few entries: the dates of his father's and mother's birth, marriage and death; then—"Oliver Wendell Holmes, b. March 8, 1841. Fanny Bowditch Dixwell, b. Dec. 12, 1840, d. April 30, 9:30 P.M. 1929."

The handwriting is very small and closely crowded, hard to decipher. In 1925 he noted "Crocuses out in White House grounds Feb. 23"; and immediately under those words—"1926—about March 20." The next year he recorded: "March 18th cherry trees by the basin in flower . . . April 12 blood root."

One quotation from his reading he copies, and jots down the date, "October 6, '85." It is from Caird's *Social Philosophy and Religion of Comte*, and must have struck him as curiously satisfying, for it afforded a bridge between his doubt as to the value of all ultimates, on the one hand, and his faith in life and in his own traditions and aspirations as an integral part of that life, on the other. The gulf between the two could not be crossed by any process of reasoning, nor by any act of faith. And yet he could not reject life, which stirred so strongly in his veins, and skepticism, carried ultimately, was no more than a rejection. The quotation from Caird expresses his solution.

All criticism of the whole system of things to which we belong is, from a truly "relative" point of view, irrational. For the critic, and the standard by which he criticizes, cannot be separated from that system. . . It has often been pointed out that a logical scepticism cannot be universal. . . Doubt must rest on a basis of certitude, or it will destroy itself. But it is not less true, though it is less frequently noticed, that all criticism of the world, while it detects evil in particular, implies an ultimate optimism. For, if such criticism pretends to be more than the utterance of the tastes and wishes of an individual, it must claim to be the expression of an objective principle—a principle which, in spite of all appearances to the contrary, is realizing itself in the world.

This does not suggest so much the dilemma between skepticism and faith as the necessary relation between criticism and optimism, a suggestion which appealed to Holmes' own compelling need for inner integration. He wanted above all to be whole. Immediately after Caird's words, Holmes adds: "I have been saying for 20 years that the sceptic cannot be a pessimist because to be a pessimist (in the philosophic sense) postulates a standard independent of the universe by which to condemn it." Caird had used the word "optimism"; and Holmes, in his own comment, first wrote "The sceptic must be an optimist"; but that went a little too far, if you were an unbeliever; and he struck out the last four words and wrote over them "cannot be a pessimist."

Holmes touched something deep in the imagination of the American people. His position in American history is secure, and he will, I am inclined to think, take his place in the line of great men whose existence symbolizes for us what we cherish and find difficult to define—Washington, modest, rugged, a man of little talk and steady action, a great soldier, patient, unswerving, faithful to details, mindful of his fences and fields, with a healthy sensuality; old Franklin, wise and worldly against his homespun pride, with his curious, experimental energy, like an American Leonardo da Vinci; Jefferson, hating kings and priests and cities which took men from the land, loving freedom and believing in the new idea of universal education; Marshall, building a nation; Lincoln, a rail splitter, growing as he lived, humorous, melancholy, tender. These great men catch and hold the national faith because they express universal aspirations, as poets and prophets and seers, what the millions whom they govern or lead yearn toward but cannot say. "The theory," as Holmes wrote, "for which Hamilton argued, and he [Marshall] decided, and Webster spoke, and Grant fought, and Lincoln died, is now our corner-stone." They understand the human need of their fellows, and somehow come to symbolize what, from generation to generation, goes into making up the national inheritance. I believe that Holmes will share this lot, and be remembered for something more universal than his contribution to law. His contribution is to American life between the Civil War and the World War, and during the next ten years. Those sixty years cover a great span of our young history—the reconstruction days, the conquering of the West, the religion of individualism, the Spanish War and our growth into an international power, the machine age, the closing of the frontiers, the World War, and the gradual shift in our point of view to a more mature social outlook.

His contribution to our law, in the great English tradition, lies in leading us back from the static position that had grown up, particularly since the Civil War, to the living approach of the common law—experimental, fluid, realistic. Holmes was in the line of the great English common-law judges.

He was the greatest judge, John Morley said, of the English-speaking world.

We shall remember Holmes for his courage, for his human understanding and simplicity, for his shafts of wit, for the integrated maturity of his life. And today, now that we are in another war, we shall remember with the most vivid sense of kinship to his spirit, his soldier's faith, expressed on a Memorial Day almost sixty years ago, that we need some teacher like war.

In this snug, over-safe corner of the world we need it, that we may realize that our comfortable routine is no eternal necessity of things, but merely a little space of calm in the midst of the tempestuous untamed streaming of the world, and in order that we may be ready for danger. We need it in this time of individualist negations . . . revolting at discipline, loving flesh-pots, and denying that anything is worthy of reverence. . . For high and dangerous action teaches us to believe as right beyond dispute things for which our doubting minds are slow to find words of proof. Out of heroism grows faith in the worth of heroism.

We shall remember, too, that beyond the will to disciplined action lay his New England faith, so that he could say that it was "not improbable that man, like the grub that prepares a chamber for the winged thing it never has seen but is to be—that man may have cosmic destinies that he does not understand. And so beyond the vision of battling races and an impoverished earth I catch a dreaming glimpse of peace."

II

THE BOSTON into which Holmes was born, on March 8, 1841, was in tempo and outlook but little different from the last days of the eighteenth century out of which New England had flowered. Henry Adams, born three years earlier, felt the handicap of arriving at the end of an era which held nothing with which to meet the days that were to come. "What could become," he asks, "of such a child of the seventeenth and eighteenth centuries, when he should wake up to find himself required to play the game of the twentieth?" His grandfather, old John Quincy Adams, the President, who was to live for another ten years, used to light his fire with a flint-and-steel which the child must have fingered. This eighteenth-century Boston was suddenly to be "cut apart" for Adams, as he put it, "by the opening of the Boston and Albany Railroad; the appearance of the first Cunard steamers in the bay; and the telegraphic messages which carried from Baltimore to Washington the news that Henry Clay and James K. Polk were nominated for the Presidency (May, 1844)."

For Holmes, who had a strong sense of the overlap of history, the Revolution was not so far behind. The house in which his father was born had been the headquarters of the Committee of Safety. His grandmother, Sarah Wendell, the only daughter of Judge Oliver Wendell of Boston, as a little girl saw the British enter the town and quarter a regiment in the Old South Church, and heard folks say that "the redcoats were coming, killing and murdering everybody as they went along." As an old lady, she told her little grandson about it. He remembered; and at eighty-three passed it along to another small boy, with that sense of the continuity of history of which I have spoken. My son, Edmund Randolph, was born about a week before the old gentleman's eightieth birthday. Three years later, when I was in Washington at the same time of the year, I sent the Justice a bunch of roses, saying on my card that it was not hard for me to remember his birthday as Randolph was eighty years younger. A few days later Randolph got this letter:

My dear Boy: Your charming nosegay speaks to me of the future. Some day you may like to remember an old man who spoke to you of the past. My grandmother died when I was fighting in the battle before Richmond in 1862. I remember her well and she remembered moving out of Boston when the British troops came in at the beginning of the Revolution. Later in London I talked with a man who had been a school mate of Lord Byron and a friend of Charles Lamb. This will mean nothing to you now, but if you remember it someday it will carry you back a good way. Meantime I thank you and hope that we may meet.

Boston was in the full bloom of her flower when Holmes was born—Van Wyck Brooks places the period from 1815 to 1865. George Ticknor, Webster, Prescott, Motley, Parkman, Longfellow, Dana, Lowell, Emerson, Hawthorne, Margaret Fuller, Thoreau, Doctor Holmes, Whittier—these are great names. "The impulse existed and the movement was real." Inevitably the impulse weakened, grew uncertain, formal, cautious, and "Indian Summer," as Mr. Brooks has called his study of the second period, set in. The men of Holmes' generation showed the drying-up process—and, doubting, they knew their own weakness. "The habit of doubt;" writes Henry Adams, "of distrusting his

own judgment and of totally rejecting the judgment of the world; the tendency to regard every
question as open; the hesitation to act except as a
choice of evils; the shirking of responsibility . . .
the horror of ennui . . ." Adams had a growing
sterility which prevented him from enjoying life,
the gift, as Holmes put it, of turning all life to
ashes. Holmes, himself deeply skeptical, never with-
drew or shrank. Henry James, who was only two
years younger than Holmes, had the same over-
rarefied shrinking from contact with his own country as Adams. Holmes thought James' recurrence to
the problem of social relations of Americans to the
Old World showed a touch of underbreeding; and
that his usual fault was to be looking too much for
his second impression. Both James and Adams distrusted the direction and value of their own society,
doubted its ultimate quality. They shrank from the
physical crudeness and rawness which had gone
into the very bone of their ancestors. "Town," says
Adams, "was winter confinement . . . straight,
gloomy streets, piled with six feet of snow in the
middle. . . The New England light is glare, and
the atmosphere harshens color." And Henry James,
as Van Wyck Brooks reminds us, through the voice

of one of his characters describes the American landscape as "very hard, very cold, very vacant . . . I had no idea how little form there was . . . I feel so undraped, so uncurtained, so uncushioned . . . A terrible crude glare is over everything . . . There is no mystery in the corners; there is no light and shade in the types."

"I think of Holmes," Owen Wister said, "as mostly keeping the doors of his sympathy open, and of Adams as mostly keeping them shut."

In 1855 Louis Agassiz, Richard H. Dana, Emerson, Benjamin Peirce, Lowell, and a few other friends founded the Saturday Club. The members dined at three o'clock on the last Saturday of each month at the Parker House. Doctor Holmes joined, and Longfellow, W. H. Prescott, Hawthorne, Whittier, Charles Eliot Norton, Charles Sumner, William Morris Hunt, Charles Francis Adams, the elder James. It was not untypical of Doctor Holmes, who had said that the "Boston State House was the hub of the Solar System," that the hotel where he lunched with the other immortals should have been otherwise known as "Will's Coffee House of Boston." Van Wyck Brooks quotes Raphael Pumpelly, on his first visit to Boston in 1865, as saying that what impressed him strongly about these men, all of them brilliant talkers, was "the fact that at two closely successive dinners the same people could keep up an equally easy current of talk through eight hours without a sign of fatigue."

Young Holmes joined the club in due course, a few years after he came back from the war.

There can be little doubt that even as a lad— long-legged and not then altogether sure of him- self, not sure of his direction, but burning with ambition—he must have seen a good deal of Emer- son, who was then in his prime. There are few ref- erences to Emerson directly, but there is a reveal- ing line in a letter to Pollock written in 1930, when Holmes was eighty-nine, his mind's eye turning back to the earlier days, even before the war. "The only firebrand of my youth that burns to me as brightly as ever is Emerson. . ." Firebrand of his youth! He can remember the emotion of Emerson long after his philosophy had faded. There was a kinship of nobility between the two men; and, al- though the younger grew to think that man was not a very important manifestation, even if he was a fact that the Cosmos had produced, and had no more particular significance, thinking coldly, than a baboon or grain of sand; yet something of the nobleness of the older man lingered from the association, some sense of the splendor and dignity of life, a knowledge that living greatly was better than being small; that, almost, one had to be great to live at all. And how like Emerson Holmes could sound, as when, for instance, writing to Pollock, he said: "Belittling arguments always have a force of their own, but you and I believe that high-mindedness is not impossible to man."

His father and Mr. Emerson were very different sorts of men, the boy knew, and he wondered about them. The "Governor" was an optimist, if you could divide people up and give them tickets that way, but Mr. Emerson went much deeper, went into the roots of human beings. But the boy could not quite understand his philosophy; it seemed all mixed up with religion, and he wasn't sure about that, wasn't sure about transcendentalism—was that the word of a philosopher or a preacher? Mr. Emerson had a prejudice against logic, which he seemed to consider a secondary process, all right for the pedant mind, but unworthy of a man who, like himself, had been fed on the cumulative humanities. Mr.

Emerson had known Coleridge and Wordsworth and Carlyle. He had come three thousand miles to see Wordsworth, and when the old bard chanted his poems to him in his garden he was at first near laughing, but then, Emerson said, "I saw that he was right and I was wrong." He held to some deep intuition—was it secret?—below the surface of the senses, that gave a perception of the ultimate truth. Of course every one in Boston was more or less of a preacher; and Mr. Emerson seemed to have his feet on the ground a good deal even if his head was in the rolling clouds. Wonderful clouds, if you let yourself go on his language, which somehow stirred you more than the other fellows who weren't so cool about it all, so coolly reasonable.

The boy wanted to know, and was curious about everything, about what started it and where it was going. But above all he wanted to know where *he* was going. He had to have something to bite on before he could feel at home with the clouds. His heart beat hard—he had to be great, maybe make a great speech, or write a great book, or be an artist . . .

One reason he had to be great was on account of the Governor. Had not the Governor become instantly famous at twenty-one when he published "Old Ironsides"? That was good stuff:

> Aye, tear her tattered ensign down!
> Long has it waved on high,
> And many an eye has danced to see
> That banner in the sky.

Ever since he had graduated from Harvard in 1829 his father had been reading the class poem (eventually there were to be forty-three out of fifty-six meetings).

The Governor was all right . . . But you couldn't be witty steadily, and it was rather ghastly to have that second help of marmalade hanging over you all the time as a reward for saying what the Governor thought was worth saying at breakfast. There were a lot of great men around Boston, and of course the Governor was a great man. Perhaps the Governor was a great man . . . But he wished he didn't have so much easy small talk for all occasions. A fellow didn't have a chance. And he didn't think the Governor was fair when he said that Wendell would never make a great speaker because his neck was too thin. He didn't mind his saying it, but it was the way he said it, turning away from a perfectly simple question, being funny instead of

sticking to the point. And those endless puns . . .
But the Governor was all right.

And when he read the Governor's piece in the
Atlantic Monthly, a few years later—that is, a few
years looking back, a good many looking forward
—he had the same sense that he had had as a child,
of the Governor's always, as it were, trying to put
him where he belonged, to keep him in the one
relationship, as a son, not as an individual human
being, not, in short, as a man. The Governor had
written about finding him in the train at Harris-
burg, after he had been wounded at the battle of
Antietam, and had described their greeting: " 'How
are you, Boy?' 'How are you, Dad?' Such are the
proprieties of life, as they are observed among us
Anglo-Saxons of the nineteenth century, decently
disguising those natural impulses . . ." He hadn't
said that, he hadn't said anything like that . . .

The good doctor had a habit of deprecating his
boy, long after the boy was grown to manhood and
had begun to show the greatness that was in him.
When Wendell graduated from the Harvard Law
School in 1866, the grand tour seemed not out of
order, and he asked his father to get him letters of

introduction from John Lothrop Motley—the
wonderful old man who had been a friend of Bis-
marck at Göttingen, an attaché to St. Petersburg
at twenty-seven; had written careless novels; had
lived in Dresden, Berlin, The Hague, Brussels, writing *The Rise of the Dutch Republic*, and was lin-
gering in Boston before finally going to England to
live. It would be nice to get letters to John Stuart
Mill and Thomas Hughes. Wendell would like to
meet the author of *Tom Brown*; and the doctor
wrote to the minister:

My son, Oliver Wendell H., Jr., now commonly
styled Lieutenant-Colonel, thinks of visiting Europe
in the course of a few months, and wants me to ask
you for a line of introduction to John Stuart Mill and
to Hughes. I give his message or request without urging it. He is a presentable youth, with fair antecedents,
and is more familiar with Mill's writings than most
fellows of his years. If it like your Excellency to send
me two brief notes for him, it would please us both,
but not if it is a trouble to you.

His father could never get away from treating
this particular son as a child, perhaps because he
felt the sense of rivalry, and defended himself by
suggesting an atmosphere of dependency between

them for the outside world to see. When his friend Mrs. Kellogg wrote to congratulate him on his son's being appointed to the Supreme Judicial Court of Massachusetts, the good doctor answered: "Thank you for all the pleasant words about the *Judge*. To *think* of it,—my little boy a Judge, and able to send me to jail if I don't behave myself!"

His mother was different. She had a great reserve of strength from which he could draw if he needed it; but there was none of the pressure against him. She knew as well as he did that he could be as great as his father. And when as a small boy he had mentioned it, his casualness overdone a little, she had said, quietly but as if there could be no discussion of it:

"Of course you could be a public speaker if you wanted to, Wendell . . ."

He loved the books she gave him as a child— *The Little Picture Bible*, *The Child's Own Book*, which had just been published in Boston, and *Peter Parley's short stories for long nights*, which his mother had given him on his fourth birthday. He wrote on the flyleaf: "O. W. Holmes, Jr., from his Mother, March 8, 1845." And then, fifty-eight years later—"My dearest book when I was a boy."

Fanny Dixwell was like his mother, like a smaller circle of his mother, and he could feel her strength, when the regiment was finally mustered in, on September 5, 1861, on their way to Washington, following the standard the Boston ladies had made and the Governor of the Commonwealth had presented to the regiment . . . Holmes knew he was coming back to Fanny Dixwell. He was not sure that she was suffering then. He was never sure in the years that followed whether she was unhappy sometimes. She was fathomless, silent where she herself counted, and could cover it all with that tumbling, enchanting talk, or hide it from him in a withdrawal that was broken only by her eyes. She need have no cause for uneasiness, he was always hers, even if sometimes he did have a flirtation with some one else. He knew that she was stronger than he, and he knew how strong he was. . .

The Civil War came suddenly, touching Holmes on the shoulder, as he walked down Beacon Street idly turning the pages of Hobbes' *Leviathan*, which he had just taken out of the Athenæum. A man he knew stopped him to say, "Holmes, you've got your first lieutenant's commission in the Twentieth"—

the Twentieth Regiment of Massachusetts Volunteer Infantry. So he took the *Leviathan* back to the library. . . When the war was over and he was reading again, and in his reading had come once more to Hobbes, he found himself with a copy of the *Leviathan* in his hand the day that Fanny accepted him. He carried the *Leviathan* back to the bookstore, now that Fanny had accepted him. . .

He must write to Mrs. Howard Kennedy about his engagement to Fanny—Mrs. Kennedy, who, on that Saturday in September, ten years ago—how long it seemed!—had taken him into her house at Hagerstown after he had been wounded in the neck at Antietam and had walked uncertainly by her gate. It was a charming old brick house, with broad verandas, large rooms with high ceilings, and wandering out-houses. It was a jolly house to be nursed in, with Mrs. Kennedy's two sisters, and a lot of children who had made a good deal of a captain, and a pretty girl from Philadelphia, Ellen Jones. He wanted Ellen Jones to know that he was engaged, so he wrote to Mrs. Kennedy:

It is with a sort of trembling that I write after such an interval to the dear and respected friend who was my good Samaritan long ago. But I must send a line to

First Lieutenant Oliver Wendell Holmes

ask your good wishes. I am engaged to Miss F. B. Dixwell who has been for many years my most intimate friend and who will now I hope soon be my wife. I am sure you will not have forgotten your sympathy for your soldier boy.

They were married three months later, on June 17, 1872. And when she could afford it Fanny bought him a first edition of the *Leviathan*.

To Holmes the war meant the spirit of conquering, of achievement, a preparation for a life of conquering, that stood in his memory for something gallant and reckless, though he knew it had been a bore and often miserable. Out of the drab of the war the ideal, the inward inspiration, grew. It was easy enough to talk high talk from the ease of comfort. "I remember just before the battle of Antietam," he wrote his young friend Dr. John C. H. Wu, in 1923, "thinking and perhaps saying to a brother officer that it would be easy after a comfortable breakfast to come down the steps of one's house pulling on one's gloves and smoking a cigar to get on to a horse and charge a battery up Beacon Street, while the ladies wave handkerchiefs from a balcony. But the reality was to pass a night on the ground in the rain with your bowels out of order and then after no particular breakfast to wade a stream and attack the enemy. That is life."

As he grew older the thought of war came to mean something precious and noble to him, a selfless surrender of individual comfort and ambition to some mystic faith that drew brave men together. He put all that he had into the war, and brought out a tempered and integrated maturity. As more and more the essence of life became for him the unending struggle, the war seemed the highest symbol of that struggle. "From the beginning, to us, children of the North, life has seemed a place hung about by dark mists, out of which come the pale shine of dragon's scales, and the cry of fighting men, and the sound of swords. Beowulf, Milton, Dürer, Rembrandt, Schopenhauer, Turner, Tennyson, from the first war-song of our race to the stall-fed poetry of modern English drawing-rooms, all have had the same vision, and all have had a glimpse of a light to be followed."

He knew what the war had done to him, when he came out of it. He could see it in the eyes of the laughing girls who smiled a little uncertainly back at the man who was no longer a boy, who had become a hero in three years. He was a man. So many people stopped halfway to manhood, and stayed half-men all their lives.

The Rebs were licked, and the time had come to build the country again. They weren't a bad lot, the Rebs, only they had to be licked. What to do?

He was mustered out on July 17, 1864, and a few weeks later he went to see Emerson at his house in Concord on the Cambridge Turnpike, sheltered by the pines that Thoreau had helped him plant in 1838.

They spent the evening together. There was still a trace in the young soldier of the old longing to be a philosopher. It had burned in his mind as an undergraduate, and he felt himself seduced again by the wonderful talk. But when at the end he closed the door he knew that such a life was not for him, and it was to be sure of that that he had come again to listen. The talk seemed more reasonable and as glowing, perhaps, because he knew now that he could not be merely a philosopher. He wanted to put his teeth into something hard and exact; to work like any one else for a living; to marry Fanny when he was earning enough. It would be a difficult world, for no one knew what would happen after the waste of war, or how soon the country could recover. But he yearned to do a real job, and not to delay the doing. He didn't want "the vulgar prosperity" that Mr. Emerson despised. Yet he knew that he couldn't pursue that evanescent magic through a lifetime, as, seated over the fire with Mr. Emerson, he listened to that stirring talk, and asked questions, and never permitted himself to yield. For in the back of his mind a hard little distrustful obstinacy rose up, as he walked out into the cool night, and the rich tones of Mr. Emerson's voice faded, and his words shrank a bit as you stripped the emotion from them. . . No, he could never be a philosopher. A scholar was different; and a scholar, as Mr. Emerson had said, has to be a man of the world, and not lose himself in schools and words and become a pedant. Mr. Emerson had said he must be a realist and a man of action, a priest of thought; the scholar and the poet and the artist alone could lead America away from this materialism that was strangling her. Perhaps some day he could speculate again about the cosmos, but not yet. . . He knew his way. His own decisions were never hard.

He may have remembered that night, or such a

night with Emerson, when, on June 30, 1886, on receiving a degree of doctor of laws from Yale, he said, at the commencement:

The power of honor to bind men's lives is not less now than it was in the Middle Ages. Now as then it is the breath of our nostrils; it is that for which we live, for which, if need be, we are willing to die. It is that which makes the man whose gift is the power to gain riches sacrifice health and even life to the pursuit. It is that which makes the scholar feel that he cannot afford to be rich.

Obviously, entering business was not for him. Medicine was a sound profession, but he wanted to achieve in a world very different from that of his father. His father had studied law but had abandoned it as a profession which split hairs. Young Wendell knew he had no more inner urge for law than for anything else, but it might prove a pathway to expression. Law might be worthy of the interest of an intelligent man, for one could look out of the window of law when one had the facts, and then begin to speculate on life and destiny. Perhaps a fellow could do a bit of tall thinking, watching from that window. He knew at least that he was an internal, not an external, man, as the surgeon of his regiment used to say, and that to him ideas were more interesting than things. The immediate object of the work would not be money. And if the law seemed but a ragbag of details, and tended, as Burke said, to sharpen the mind only by narrowing it, yet what a challenge to the practical philosopher! For law is human, a part of man and of man's world, a history of the moral development of the race. . . You would have to do the job alone, but it would be worth doing. You could show each case to be in the great line of the universal.

III

Holmes entered the Harvard Law School in September, and graduated two years later, in 1866; was admitted to the bar in 1867, practiced briefly with his brother, Edward Jackson Holmes, and finally joined the firm of Shattuck, Holmes and Munroe.

His intimacy with William James began at Harvard, where James was studying science. During the winter of 1866–1867 the two friends spent many an evening together, wrangling over philosophy. Holmes was the only fellow James cared anything about. James considered him a "first-rate article," which improved by wear, even if he was "too exclusively intellectual." James had just become acquainted (in 1866) with Miss Fanny Dixwell, of Cambridge, and thought her "decidedly A1 and (so far) the best girl I have known." Thus he expresses himself to his friend, Tom Ward. A week before in similar vein he wrote his brother Wilky: "She is about as fine as they make 'em." But—"That villain Wendell Holmes has been keeping her all to himself out at Cambridge for the last eight years; but I hope I may enjoy her acquaintance now. She is A1, if anyone ever was . . ." He realized, of course, that Wendell had had more experience with the fair sex, and he seemed to have a sort of lien on Miss Dixwell. . . Three years later, writing to his brother Henry from Cambridge, William reports: "Wendell Holmes comes out and we jaw once a week. I have been out two or three times in a buggy with Miss Fanny Dixwell, and derived no mean amount of joy therefrom."

In April, 1867, James sailed for Europe, on the *Great Eastern;* but just before sailing sent a line to his friend—"Dear Wendy boy,—I will go in tomorrow night and we will evolve cosmos out of chaos for positively the last time."

But philosophy was soon to be behind Wendell, who was plunging into his immediate work. In September William wrote him from Berlin, complaining of his friend's silence and asking after their "dilapidated old friend the Cosmos." Wendell wrote William on December 15 of the same year that "for two or three months I debauched o' nights in philosophy. But now it is law—law— law." He had written three long letters that winter to his friend, but had destroyed them, he said, as they seemed unsound or incomplete, until Fanny Dixwell had told him to fire away anyhow. He felt alone in his thoughts and inner feelings, in spite of his friends. And writing James gave him, he confessed, a secret comfort and companionship. He was reading Kant's *Critique of Pure Reason*, and discoursed on the categories, though he was no logician, and thought it all "puerile stuff enough . . . to waste energy on. But it seems necessary to read a good deal of useless stuff, in order to know that it is so and not to depend only on a surmise." Reinforcing his intuitions, he might have said. And, too, he was "reading Tyndall's book on *Heat*— what a yellow-whiskered, healthy, florid-complected, pleasant English book it is, to be sure." He had met an Englishman, a Mr. Henry Cowper, who "had the cosmos at heart, and we hammered at it late into the night several times . . ."

This letter crossed one from his friend, now in Berlin, trying hard to read, a little lonely, unable to sleep, so that he writes: "I clutch the pen and ink and resolve to work off the fit by a few lines to one of the most obtrusive ghosts of all—namely the tall and lank one of Charles Street. Good golly!" he cries, "how I would prefer to have about twenty-four hours' talk with you up in that whitely lit-up room—without the sun rising or the firmament revolving so as to put the gas out, without sleep, food, clothing or shelter except your whiskey bottle. . . I have been chewing on two or three dried-up old cuds of ideas I brought from America with me, till they have disappeared, and the nudity of the Kosmos has got beyond anything I have as yet experienced. . . I don't know how it is I am able to take so little interest in reading this winter. . . I have reached an age when practical work of some kind clamors to be done—and I must still wait!"

Four months later spring had come to Boston —if April in Boston can be called spring—and Wendell in a long letter to Bill tells him about it. The letter is a charming combination of poetry, sentimentality, and humor. The style has a youthful self-consciousness about it, is free and incisive only in spots, but these are telling; and we get a sense that it is hard to hold to the lonely task while spring is outside the window calling. "The icy teeth have melted out of the air and winter has snapped at us for the last time. Now are the waters beneath

my window of a deeper and more significant blue
than heretofore. Now do the fields burn with green
fire—the evanescent hint of I know not what hidden longing of the earth. Now all the bushes bur-
geon with wooly buds and the elm trees have put
on bridal veils of hazy brown." That is almost too
much, and he adds to a chorus of frogs, answering
a chorus of birds, the wandering couples who after
sunset "draw near to each other in the dark spaces
between the gas lights and think themselves un-
seen." Cambridge is "filled with collegians with
new hats and sticks and shining schoolboy faces."
How old he must have felt, and with what charming youthfulness he turns to Bill, "to thee, not with
more affection than during the long grind of the
winter, but desiring if it may be to say a word to
thee once more."

It is all very much in the style of the times and
of his own recent manhood. He assures Bill that
"philosophy has hibernated in torpid slumber, and
I have lain 'sluttishly soaking and gurgling in the
devil's pickle,' as Carlyle says. It has been necessary,—if a man chooses a profession he cannot forever content himself in picking out the plums with
fastidious dilettantism . . . but must eat his way

manfully through crust and crumb—soft, unpleasant, inner parts which, within one, swell, causing discomfort in the bowels." He was conscious, as he wrote, of his fear of being a dilettante, like his father, of knowing the temptation that sat near his elbow to level phrases at the cosmos. You mustn't skim the cream from a book, but must hold it till it is done, cover to cover, taking the dull stretches with the higher vistas. The idea pursued him through life, and we find him reading with a sort of fierce sense of duty, and groaning in his letters to friends over some book that it would be shirking to put down.

But he does not want Bill to think the winter has not been a success. The discipline of the work has increased his "conviction that law as well as any other series of facts in this world may be approached in the interests of science and may be studied, yes and practiced, with the preservation of one's ideals. I should even say that they grew robust under the regimen,—more than that I do not ask." One cannot finish the search of mankind, as one might have reached to do when young, but must reconcile oneself to life. But there are "vanishing points which give a kind of perspective to the chaos of events

. . . to dimly apprehend that this dream disturbing the sleep . . . is well—to suspect some of the divine harmonies, though you cannot note them like a score of music . . ."

Unusual music for a boy of twenty-seven, writing as the New England winter broke outside his window. . .

In the next paragraph of this extraordinary letter he slides back, with folded wings, into a young-man-about-town pose. Unlike Harry James, who never lets up on his high aims, he admits that "I *do*. There are not infrequent times when a bottle of wine, a good dinner, a girl of some trivial sort can fill the hour for me."

At the end he comes back to "the mighty quickening of the spring."

The larches have sprouted.
I saw a butterfly today just loosed from the bondage of winter, and a bee toiling in sticky buds half opened. . .
A keen, slender, stridulous vibration—almost too fine for the hearing, weaving in and out, and in the pauses of the music dividing the silence like a knife—pierces my heart with an ecstasy I cannot utter. . .
Dear Bill, to whom should I vent this madness but to you?

He held the letter for a week, and added a postscript. "It is snowing again. S'help me."

William answered the following May, thrilled with the "impact" of the letter. He thought a good five hours' talk with Holmes would probably do him more good than almost any other experience he could conceive of. For "in personal contact, Wendell, lies a deep dark power . . . The fact is, my dear boy, that I feel more as if you were my ally against what you call 'the common enemy' than any one I know."

When William returned from Europe the familiar intimacy continued. "W. Holmes rings the bell as usual at eight and one-half o'clock on Saturday evenings," Mrs. James writes her son Henry, "and we are all falling into our old ways." But there was a difference that each of the young men sensed. Holmes seemed to his friend to have become harder, more ironical and self-centered. Had the law done something to him? Holmes was a baffling fellow. "I have seen no one else of any interest except Wendell Holmes and John Gray," James wrote his friend Tom Ward. "They are such first-class minds, and I like them so much personally, that I deeply regret that they should be getting more and more absorbed in legal business and study whereby the sympathies we have in common are growing very narrowed." He missed in his dealing with Wendell the body of common interests he had with medical men. "The mystery of the *Total* is a rather empty platform to be the only one to meet a man on. . ."

And to the young lawyer the young philosopher lacked firmness and direction. But what an impulsive, lovable, selfless cuss he was, even if at times he seemed lost in a dreamy cloud of optimism!

William worried about Wendell, and wrote Henry P. Bowditch, who had been with him in the Medical School: "Wendell Holmes pays me a weekly visit. John Ropes (a fellow student of Holmes and John C. Gray at the law school) told me the other night he had never known of anyone in the law who studied anything like as hard as Wendell. (This must lead to Chief Justice, U. S. Supreme Court.) Wendell amuses me by being composed of at least two and a half different people rolled into one, and the way he keeps them together in one tight skin, without quarreling any more than they do, is remarkable. I like him and esteem him exceedingly . . ." The next week

James reported to his brother Henry: "Wendell Holmes has skipped many Saturdays often by my request, but comes pretty regular. He is very affectionate *to* me and *of* you. . . I think he improves surely every year, and has that in him which makes you sure his fire won't burn out before the age of thirty, as most everyone else's seems to. . ." A few months later James again wrote Bowditch from Pomfret, Connecticut: "Wendell Holmes and John Gray were on here last Saturday and Sunday, and seemed in very jolly spirits at being turned out to pasture from their Boston pen. I should think Wendell worked too hard. Gray is going to Lenox for a fortnight, but W. is to take no vacation." He had undertaken a two years' job to edit the twelfth edition of Kent's *Commentaries*, and was so "ambitious of excellence," that he told his friend that the time was too short for the amount of work he was resolved to put into it, and it weighed heavy on his soul. . .

Yet Wendell's egotism shocked his friend's sensitive nature. "The more I live in the world," William wrote Henry, "the more cold-blooded, conscious egotism and conceit of people afflict me. . . All the noble qualities of Wendell Holmes, for instance, are poisoned by them, and friendly as I want to be towards him, as yet the good he has done me is more in presenting me something to kick away from or react against than to follow and embrace . . ." Holmes was strong medicine, even at twenty-eight.

They were all concerned about the young scholar, who was almost haggard with work. In 1873 Mrs. James reported to Henry:

> Wendell Holmes dined with us a few days ago. His whole life, soul and body, is utterly absorbed in his *last* work upon his Kent. He carries about his manuscript in his green bag and never loses sight of it for a moment. He started to go to Will's room to wash his hands, but came back for his bag, and when we went to dinner, Will said, "Don't you want to take your bag with you?" He said, "Yes, I always do so at home." His pallid face, and this fearful grip upon his work, makes him a melancholy sight.

James occasionally went to stay with Holmes after his friend's marriage to Miss Dixwell. He found him growing more and more concentrated upon his law, sometimes feeling the effects of overwork, his mind like a stiff spring that flew tight back the instant it was left to itself. She exerted the old charm. . . Holmes was "a powerful battery, formed like a planing machine to gouge a deep self-beneficial groove through life. . ."

In the fifteen years before he went on the bench Holmes got the feel of practice, the healthy rub with men who were very active at the bar. He was connected in one way or another with thirty-four cases before the Supreme Judicial Court of Massachusetts, appearing as counsel alone in nine, as senior in twelve, and as associate in the others.

Sidney Bartlett was at his height, a great advocate come down from the eighteenth century. Holmes, cherishing the sense of history, told of a letter of Bartlett which ran—"Deacon Spooner died in 1818 aged ninety-four. I saw him and talked with him. *He* talked with Elder Faunce, who talked with the Pilgrims and is said to have pointed out *the* rock." Bartlett had died at ninety, two months after arguing two cases before Holmes' court with unabated fire. "He had," Holmes said in an address to the bar, "that terse and polished subtilty of speech which was most familiar to the world where courtiers and men of fashion taught the *littérateurs* of a later age how to write. He had something of the half-hidden wit which men learned to practice who lived about a court and had to speak in innuendo. He had much of the eighteenth century definiteness of view which was such an aid to perfection of form." The words might have been written about Holmes himself.

Holmes liked to remember William M. Evarts' remark about Bartlett. Evarts was another legal giant of Holmes' youth. Bartlett had referred to the "thin thread of thought" in one of Evarts' arguments. Evarts later had said to a group of lawyers: "Here comes Bartlett, trying to decide whether he made God or God made him."

Holmes had a profound admiration for George Otis Shattuck, in whose office he had begun work; and Shattuck will be remembered by what Holmes said about him in answer to resolutions of the bar in 1897. "He needed the excitement of advocacy or of some practical end to awaken his insight, but when it was awakened there was no depth of speculation or research which he was not ready and more than able to sound . . . He had learned the all too rarely learned lesson of pointed brevity. In a few luminous words he went to the bottom of his question, and then took his seat . . . What we have done," he concluded, "is woven forever into the great vibrating web of the world. The eye that can read the import of its motion can decipher the story of all our deeds, of all our thoughts. To that eye I am content to leave the recognition and the memory of this great head and heart."

Louis D. Brandeis was admitted to practice in 1878, and Holmes at once recognized his ability, and asked him to spend an evening or two to discuss some of the theoretical aspects of the law of torts—a subject about which he had been doing a good deal of speculation. The two men, so different in outlook and temperament, became lifelong friends. As they grew older, and their lives crossed again in Washington, Holmes felt the sort of reverence for the younger man—ascetic, Spartan, desperately in earnest—that one might have for a friendly saint with a crusading spirit. "Whenever he left my house," Holmes wrote of him in 1932, "I was likely to say to my wife, 'There goes a really good man.' . . In the moments of discouragement that we all pass through, he always has had the happy word that lifts up one's heart. It came from knowledge, experience, courage, and the high way in which he always has taken life."

In the first few years after his graduation from the law school, Holmes was deep in his reading, in the small room in the garret of the house his father had built at 296 Beacon Street, overlooking the Charles River. He was teaching constitutional law at Harvard in 1870, and at the same time writing a good many articles and editorials for the *American Law Journal*. He edited Kent's *Commentaries* seven years after he had been out of college. The Lowell lectures on the common law in 1880 and 1881 led to his great book, *The Common Law*, published the latter year. The lectures had impressed his hearers as an extraordinary intellectual performance. He had been casual, easy, as if "reasoning at the moment" out of the richness of a subject which was a part of him, so thoroughly had he mastered it, and they knew it was no mere matter of memory.

IV

He was careful to get the last proof of *The Common Law* to the printer before March 8; to date the preface, Boston, February 8, 1881. What Frenchman had said that every great man will show his greatness before reaching forty? He remembered that he had made a rash promise to his old friend Mrs. Owen Wister of Philadelphia—that charming daughter of Fanny Kemble and Pierce Butler, whose son was then a junior at Harvard—that when he published a book he would send her a copy. In sending it he wrote her: "But for that promise I should not have ventured to do so as the contents are not of a kind which I can hope you will find interesting. But I hereby exonerate you from all obligation to look into it further than to admit that it is pretty well printed and ask you to accept it simply as a mark of homage." She pasted his letter in the front of *The Common Law*, and put the book in the library at Butler Place. He was rather awed by Mrs. Wister. She had about her the grace and style of the *grandes dames* of an earlier century, so that he could write her a few years later with a sense of the appropriateness of the expression: "I dined with Mrs. Warren on Wednesday who still had the scent of the roses of her visit hanging round her and made me feel as if I had been near you."

The object of the book was to present a general review of the common law; and if within these bounds he were reproached "for a want of greater detail," he could "only quote the words of Lehuërou, 'Nous faisons une théorie et non un spicilège.' " "To accomplish the task," he wrote, "other tools are needed besides logic. It is something to show that the consistency of a system requires a particular result, but it is not all. The life of the law has not been logic: it has been experience. The felt necessities of the time, the prevalent moral and political theories, institutions of public policy, avowed or unconscious, even the prejudices which judges share with their fellow-men, have had a good deal more to do than the syllogism in determining the rules by which men should be governed. The law embodies the story of a nation's development through many centuries, and it cannot be dealt with as if it contained only the axioms and corollaries of a book of mathematics. In order to know what it is, we must know what it has been, and what it tends to become . . . The substance of the law at any given time pretty nearly corresponds, so far as it goes, with what is then understood to be convenient; but its form and machinery, and the degree to which it is able to work out desired results, depend very much upon its past."

That is the opening of *The Common Law*, and affords insight into the approach which was thereafter to guide Holmes' thinking. The approach was historic, eclectic, experimental. It viewed the symbols which for so many had represented an established order, and penetrated far below and behind their glittering aspect of the eternal to find the psychologic or convenient reason which had conditioned their origin. The scholar, as Emerson had said, must be a man of the world. And as law is but an expression of the ebb and flow of life, it must seek vitality in that unending movement of the stream. "The truth is," Holmes writes, still in the first chapter, "that the law is always approaching, and never reaching, consistency. It is forever adopting new principles from life at one end, and it always retains old ones from history at the other, which have not yet been absorbed or sloughed off. It will become entirely consistent only when it ceases to grow."

Thus the modern law of liability has its roots in the law of revenge, "vengeance, not compensation, and vengeance on the offending thing," and stems from a moral basis, an immensely significant discovery if we are to understand the law of tort and of crime. And yet historical explanations are insufficient, for the "growth of the law is legislative . . . in its grounds. The very considerations which judges most rarely mention, and always with an apology, are the secret root from which the law draws all the juices of life . . . considerations of what is expedient for the community concerned . . . the unconscious result of instinctive preferences and inarticulate convictions, but none the less traceable to views of public policy in the last analysis."

For so many years now these considerations have been so much a part of our critical approach to law, whether or not all of us acknowledge their inevitable truth, that it is difficult today to realize how revolutionary they sounded in a country still absorbed in the worship of courts, and happy in the naïve assumption that law, which after all had been written on the sacred tablets, was a complete and perfected system, as authoritative and as ineluctable as morals, on whose broad but clear precepts, after all, it was firmly founded!

The discovery that judges are human beings and act accordingly in a world of law, trying to keep up with the constantly changing world of life—or, perhaps more accurately, the rediscovery and application—came as a shock to the bar and the bench, and for that matter to the public, who liked to insist on keeping their judges symbols of the mechanical perfection which life did not vouchsafe to laymen. They never stopped to wonder how the brief ceremony of induction could endow the incumbent with that perfection; as one of Willa Cather's characters, an old Negro servant, watching the wedding ceremony of white folks, wondered how so brief a performance could change what before was altogether wrong into what now was altogether right. The law was there to expound not to create, they argued, remembering that Blackstone had written that judges are "not delegated to pronounce a new law, but to maintain and expound the old law." As late as 1905 John C. Carter was insisting that the function of the judge was not to make but to discover law. And Calvin Coolidge added: "Men do not make laws. They do but discover them . . . That state is most fortunate in its form of government which has the aptest instruments for the discovery of laws." Chancellor Kent had been franker, a century earlier. He first made himself "master of the facts." Then—"I saw where justice lay, and the moral sense decided the court half the time; I then sat down to search the authorities . . . I might once in a while be embarrassed by a technical rule, but I almost always found principles suited to my view of the case."

Perhaps if we had not inherited our law, as we inherited our language, our traditions, and our memories from an older country the formalism that settled over its expression would have left less rigid marks. The colonial mind, limited by the unknown frontier crowding the border of its frail civilization, turned instinctively to the mother country to fortify itself with the dimming memories of the rituals that had been left behind. Inevitably the reason for the symbols fades; yet the shell of the ancient tradition, growing dimmer, is more ardently admired. Form remains where substance has gone. It is no wonder, therefore, that Blackstone appealed to the young nation, in its pioneer psychology, as a counsel of perfection more readily accepted in the nostalgia of remembrance. Otherwise it is difficult to explain, particularly to the foreigner who expects a greater freedom from convention in this new and, in some respects, unconventional country, the veneration which Americans pay to doctrinaire absolutes that often do not seem to fit their different needs; the passion for completed systems; the belief that eternals can be written down on paper for guides forever to future generations.

Across this static concept that was blocking change and making law curiously outmoded and unexpressive of the hurried life that swept about it the impact of Holmes' stalwart genius swept with the vigor of a fresh and salty wind. We had got away from the great tradition of English common law; and it was his achievement to break down the walls of formalism and empty traditionalism which had grown up around the inner life of the law in America. His acute scholarship searched the reason for the rules, that, as he said, like the clavicle of the cat had become obsolete; he went beyond the mumbled legal phrases that had dammed up thinking for so long; and his humanity afforded a link between that scholarship and the functional world that he saw about him.

What Holmes insisted on in *The Common Law* he continued to say for the next fifty years in his opinions, and in those rare and tantalizingly brief speeches, his "chance utterances of faith and doubt," and the occasional articles which, in the preface to his *Collected Legal Papers* he called "little fragments of my fleece that I have left upon the hedges of life." As a great legal historian he knew that "a page of history is worth a volume of logic." But though "the past gives us our vocabulary and fixes the limits of our imagination . . . the present has a right to govern itself so far as it can; and it ought always to be remembered that historic continuity with the past is not a duty, it is only a necessity." History "is the first step toward an enlightened scepticism, that is, towards a deliberate reconsideration of the worth of . . . rules . . . It is revolting to have no better reason for a rule of law than that so it was laid down in the time of Henry IV. It is still more revolting if the grounds upon which it was laid down have vanished long since, and the rule simply persists from blind imitation of the past." If you leave the path of logical deduction, "you lose the illusion of certainty which makes legal reasoning seem like mathematics."

"I cannot but believe," he said in a speech, "that if the training of lawyers led them habitually to consider more definitely and explicitly the social advantage on which the rule they lay down must be justified, they sometimes would hesitate where now they are confident, and see that really they were taking sides upon debatable and often burning questions."

Jerome Frank, in his book *Law and the Modern Mind*, which draws greatly on Holmes' approach to law, believes that he "almost alone among lawyers, adopts that skeptical attitude upon which modern science has builded, that modern skepticism which looks upon thought as instrumental and acknowledges the transient and relative nature of all human thought-contrivances." That view requires courage to face the fact that "men have made the law and must take the responsibility for its good or bad workings." Law can never be perfect; and it is that honest admission that makes Holmes a vital and progressive skeptic, emotionally adult in the life of the law.

Max Lerner, in an article written after Holmes' death, makes a similar reflection that what most clearly emerges as one reads Holmes is that he was a whole man, that his genius proceeded not from eccentricity or from revolt, but from the flowering of the New England intellectual aristocracy. I suspect that Holmes' eager appetite for life, and the single direction of his unshaken will more nearly accounted for what he was than his Brahmin background. Lerner thought Holmes could never rid himself of the influence of Plato, that he still lived in the realm of the essences. But to Holmes the universal was an illusion, even if facts had to be sifted through its aspect, in order to deal at all with the chaos of life. Lerner suggests, too, that Holmes was ridden by the leisure-class myths of the soldier and of the gambler. The words describe much that was in him; but they evoke characteristics common to all mankind. And if the eternal struggle seemed to him the basis of life—and he was all for taking risks rather than weighing them —those instincts never diverted his will or bent his path. And finally Lerner concludes that, even if Holmes maintained the great aristocratic tradition, "his influence lingers only with a few dissenters, protesting in a diminuendo. The prevailing tone of style and thought in the Supreme Court decisions is now set by Justice McReynolds and Justice Sutherland." These words were written about a year after Holmes was dead. In another year Sutherland, McReynolds, Butler and Van Devanter were dissenting, often bitterly, as in the Gold Clause Cases, talking of the "spoliation of citizens," and of "the impending legal and moral chaos." And in 1941 Mr. Justice Holmes' dissent in *Hammer* v. *Dagenhart* had become the law.

V

HOLMES WAS appointed to the Supreme Judicial
Court of Massachusetts on December 15, 1882, and
took his seat nineteen days afterward. He had been
teaching constitutional law and torts at the Harvard Law School, and President Eliot and Professor Ames wanted him to stay on. Here was his
métier, they urged, the life of a scholar for which
he was pre-eminently fitted, as he had shown by
editing the *Commentaries* and writing *The Common Law*. But he did not hesitate. Here was a
chance to see reality unfold before him, so that
perhaps he might discover the rhythmic unplanned
mystery that lay behind. That could not be found
in the comfortable continuity of the student's
closet. It was one thing to utter a happy phrase
from a protected cloister. The final measure of men
lay in the human energy which they embodied,
whether in battle or the market place or the court.
The past was but a guide to the future, and the
great problems were questions of here and now.

Besides, he knew the past, and longed to broaden the canvas of the pressing life of every day, about which he was intensely curious, and ponder the stream of experience. Surely the bench would afford an opportunity of watching that stream, of noting its direction, perhaps, even, of influencing it.

It is difficult to appraise the twenty years that Holmes spent on the state court. I am tempted to think that relatively he did not greatly grow in stature during that period. He needed a broader field and richer contacts from which to unfold the insight that later marked the expression of his genius. Boston was settled, self-centered, and patronizing about Wendell Holmes, whom no one could take quite seriously. The sense of the past hung over the present, and men were concerned with remembering what had gone rather than making the future. The great men had died, or, like the good doctor, would die some day. The younger men were moving away to New York or to the West, and the weaker among them, who had remained, were unable to shake off the settled past enough to accept the new culture, crude, perhaps, but more vigorous than a memory. They did not know that the eighteenth century had gone; and expressed their diminishing power by hating the Irish Catholics, the new invaders, and by exercising their resistance in the feeble protest of reformers. Nor did they know that a very great man was living in their town, who would turn all the power of that past, their own New England blood, which ran so straight from the blood of old England, into creative insight to understand and interpret the New America that was growing up about them.

Holmes was hungry for the adventure of greatness. He knew he had the seeds of greatness in him. He knew and he was lonely, feeling alone and with a shadow of melancholy in a world where, after all, he and his father's fathers had been born and bred. So many of these fellows used the lazy makeshift of mumbling over the familiar, living in a routine which they themselves invoked by not exercising their powers in the present. They rested upon the slumber of formulas which pointed in the direction of death. Not that he did not have a sense of the past, that essential feeling of the overlap of time, or that he was not, to his marrow and bone, a New Englander. . . Fanny, too, who had sea captains in her family, and loved the sea, and the quiet little white churches, and elms nodding along the ordered streets and unassuming commons. She executed a carved wooden panel representing the sea breaking over a hatchway with a spar afloat, which they gave to the town of Gloucester. For the inscription she chose an epitaph in the Greek Anthology:

> A shipwrecked sailor buried on this coast
> Bids thee take sail.
> Full many a gallant ship, when we were lost,
> Weathered the gale.

Together they walked and drove a good deal. He liked to gaze over the lonely cliffs to the sea beyond, then drive along the crowded beaches, skirt the windswept downs and follow the little inland farms which ran down to the marshy inlets of Ipswich or Pride's Crossing.

Young Owen Wister was in Boston a good deal after he graduated from college in 1882. He was at the Harvard Law School from 1885 to 1888, and was constantly at the Holmes house at 9 Chestnut Street. He was handsome, and with his quick and witty talk, his sense of gusto and a keen enjoyment of life, brought to the soberer background of Puritan New England a fleeting note of sensuousness and gaiety. There was no doubt that he was having a good time; and the Judge enjoyed it, a little vicariously perhaps, for he knew he was firmly settled in the straight path of accomplishment, which apparently in order to be straight had also to be narrow. So he writes to Wister, in 1886: "I almost was with you myself when I read your letter (which I burned at once as you directed). Larks still are, if I *am* sitting in a murder trial. Come when you can and feel like it."

It was with a little hesitation that he asked the young blade, a few months later, to dine with him "at the vile hour of 2 ½ at Parker's Pot House tomorrow with the Saturday Club, which is supposed to consist of great swells, and is sometimes pleasant and not infrequently dull . . ." He would write him "to signify that your rights in 1 bot. (contents and value unknown but believed great) Hungarian wine—the bottle being of Rhein wine fashion, also in the stock of Great Western now on hand, expire at the end of dinner time on Sunday eve next." Wister would send him French plays and novels.

"I have got Madame Cardinal from the Ath.m,"
Holmes writes him, "and am reading it with much
amusement. Don't bring me in the other books
unless you solemnly take on yourself the burden of
removing them. I can get them—and books bor-
rowed from friends weigh on my soul like lead."
But Wister doubted whether he could get some of
them, at least from the Athenæum, and kept on
sending them.

In the spring of 1889 Holmes was planning a trip
to England. His sister had died, and it was settled
that they were to live with his father. It was the
only practical thing, he supposed. But he felt somewhat collapsed and flat, and fell in with the idea
when Fanny suggested he should go abroad, that it
would make the summer easier for the Governor.
They had been saving to go to Europe together.
There was not enough money for both of them to
go, but there was enough for one, and she had insisted that it must be he, that he should seize the
chance now that it was here, for it might not come
again for a long time. You couldn't change Fanny,
once she had made up her mind; and such great
decisions, somehow, were in her province.

It would be fun to get Wister to go along; and

he wrote the younger man, a little shyly: "It has occurred to me as a pleasing dream that if you were going the same way we might go together coalescing or separating at moments if desirable so as not to impair each other's freedom and yet gaining much happiness—on my side at least." He added: "By May I suppose I shall be in father's house, where Mrs. Holmes has been from before my sister's death. So that among other inconveniences I shall have no spare room—but we can make shift to have as much time together as you can spare or I err." Perhaps neither father nor son was particularly pleased at the prospect of living together, but each made the best of it. Doctor Holmes, who was almost eighty, wrote to his friend Mrs. Ward, the day before his son's letter to Wister:

I am not left alone. My daughter-in-law, a very helpful, hopeful, powerful as well as brilliant woman, is with me, and my household goes on smoothly, and not without a cheerful aspect. Her husband the Judge will soon be established in the house, and I trust we shall live as happily as we ought to, if my large allowance of years should be a little farther extended.

A powerful and brilliant woman hardly sounds comfortable; but experience proved the contrary;

and two years later, the old gentleman, who, like his son, was an inveterate letter writer, tells Mrs. Kellogg that "Mrs. Judge knows how to make me comfortable, and does it wonderfully well."

But Wister held out for his independence, and Holmes went alone to England that summer, where he saw Henry James. Alice, Henry's sister, who was then living in England to try to recover her failing health, makes this entry in her journal.

H. [her brother, Henry] says that W. H. [Wendell Holmes] has had a most brilliant success in London, and that he was as pleasant as possible, young-looking, and handsomer than ever,—flirting as desperately too. I suppose that his idea of "heaven" is still "flirting with pretty girls," as he used to say. This that he said once still survives in my mind: "Every man sees something of Mrs. Nickleby in his own mother" . . . I remember the torpid A. G. Sedgwick telling me one day that he had gone to a telegraph office, written his message, and handed it to the clerk, whom he asked "Is it plain?" "Plain, but peculiar." O. W. H. said that the absence of such possibilities is what makes one so homesick in Europe, to the disgust of the offended Arthur.

Holmes' brief letters to Wister over their years of friendship are written with a sense of irresponsibility in the relationship. "I am as busy as a witch in a gale of wind," Holmes writes, "and must go out to catch a man to dine with. A Britoness tomorrow night—would you were here." He never called him Owen, usually "Wister," or "Whisker." "The amount of vexation you cause me by not being on hand when wanted is inconsistent Wisker friend." He invariably signed himself "affectionately," or the like.

Holmes disliked interrupting the routine of his court work; and when Wister asked him to spend a week-end at Butler Place, Philadelphia, he was torn between this disinclination and the temptation to visit again that charming spot. He thought he should decline, he wrote his friend. He didn't like to promise so long beforehand. There was an ever imminent probability of something turning up which needed him at home. He was in "abject confusion" because he might be hailed for a speech. He had had a "steady drain upon my intellectuals," and so shrank from anything he could lawfully avoid. Big functions always made him blue and wore on his nerves. But he was tempted— Three weeks later he made up his mind to go. Fanny had told him he was an old fuss and ought to get away from the court and freshen up, and she would look after things at home. He wrote to ask at what station he was to get off, he was confused. But he wasn't good for a speech. He doubted whether he could drink any wine. He had been at it too hard. . . If the Colonial was late don't wait dinner for me. He would be in despair if he gave trouble to Mrs. Wister. . . He assumed from Wister's silence that there was but one station, so that his innocent feet would not be led astray. "My father always used to caution me if an old woman with an orange approached not to follow her."

Wister had written a few short stories; and in 1892 wrote Holmes he was sending him his first book, *The Dragon of Wantley*. "I await the dragon," Holmes writes him, "with feelings not unlike the knight in the last *Fliegende Blätter*. A gallant crusader can't get a light for his pipe from the passerby so he goes to the dragon's den and when the beast opens a pit of spouting flame upon him he catches a spark, says thank you very much —and walks off again. The parallel is obvious. . . I also have done my usual modicum of philosophic, economic and historical reading." The reading for the year 1892 listed in the black book includes some seventy-nine books. Among the philosophic are James' *Psychology*, Royce's *Spirit of Modern Philosophy*, Lotze's *Outlines of Metaphysic, Practical Philosophy*, and *Psychology*. For the economic, Gibbins' *Industrial History of England*, Robertson's *Fallacy of Saving*, and (again) *The Leviathan*. Fanny had read aloud Barrie's *Little Minister* and *When a Man's Single*, Daudet's *Rose et Ninette*, Mark Twain's *Merry Tales*. He had tried a good deal of French in the first part of the year—Gyp's *Monsieur Fred*, Catulle Mendès' *Jupe Courte*, Marcel Prévost's *La Confession d'un amant*. The same author's *Lettres de femmes* was followed by Hegel's *Logic* . . .

I have convinced myself once more [continues his letter to Wister] that whatever Hegel may have started he had a deal of the charlatan in him and as a *result* is no good. I have wondered whether Royce knows any more about the world outside of space time and causation than I do. . . I have seen the *verae causae* of events in a little industrial history of England better worth reading than all the big books and also have pursued like themes on a larger scale. I have rebelled and thanked God that man was an animal capable of denying the industrial order and doing the spontaneous uneconomic thing. . . I have reperused

my friend Pulszky's book on the Theory of Law, etc.
—also a dish of Roman law, and have wound up on
Blaine's *20 years in Congress* which (esp. Vol. 1) to
my mind is a work of profound dramatic interest,
most ably done, and among other things a valuable
cure to anyone who has any sentimental tendencies
toward England. . . I grow more and more a re-
cluse [it would be ten years more before he left
Boston]. I think most of the society women here-
abouts empty humbugs (this with bated breath—not
to be repeated) and besides I am not able to dine
out. . .

He thinks Wister's friend Jack Chapman's piece
about Abbott and Royce pretty thin, with a *"tête
montée* quality which I should think his friends
would prefer to suppress." From some of Chapman's verses Holmes felt that the iron had entered
into his soul, and he was to be pitied, not criticised.
"Indeed that is my final bottom feeling about anyone—but one can't let it be his official attitude."
He ends: "I feel successful, old and reasonably resigned." He was fifty-one.

His father died on October 7, 1894. Two days
later Sir Frederick Pollock expressed his sympathy
to Holmes in these words: "I cannot bring myself

to apply the common terms of lamentation to the close of one of the longest, most complete, most beneficent and I think I cannot be wrong in saying happiest lives of this century..." Holmes answered: "I face rather solemnity than sadness. My father had had all that he could have from life and he quietly ceased breathing as Mrs. Holmes and I stood by his side... The marks which I have seen of universal affection for him here and a widespread similar feeling with you give me much pleasure."

L'Echo de la Semaine, in a long article, found in the Autocrat a happy mixture of humor and sentiment. *C'est lui*, it remarked, *qui, plaisamment, baptisa Boston l'essieu du monde.* New England, the writer concluded, was the narrow cradle of American civilization and genius. *La mort de Holmes marque la fin d'une brillante période d'écrivains à laquelle appartenaient, à côté de Longfellow et de Lowell, Whittier, le poète quaker de l'émancipation des noirs, le philosophe Emerson, et tant d'autres noms éminents que nous pourrions citer sans sortir de la Nouvelle-Angleterre, cet étroit berceau de la civilisation et du génie américain, ce petit point sur le littoral de l'Atlantique qui est comme l'âme de la nation.*

The Judge knew himself a New Englander, deep beneath the wider culture, the easier gait, which life had brought him. His stock was New England to the core—soldiers, clergymen, judges. Mrs. Temperance Holmes, his great-grandmother, was typical of her sturdy time and race. Her son had recorded in his diary, soon after her death in 1803, that she had eight children, and "to the affairs of her household she was assiduously and unweariedly attentive, and never ate the bread of idleness . . ." The diary also expressed the writer's admiration for his grandmother, Mrs. Temperance Hewet, who possessed very superior accomplishments. "She had a thirst for knowledge; so desirous was she of knowing something of Virgil in the original, that, with some little instruction and the aid of a dictionary, she examined that classical author for herself."

That was it, a thirst for knowledge; and the instinct for caution which he had inherited from his great-great-grandmother, Temperance Hewet, that was in the very flow of his blood, and dictated the thriftiness which seemed to him so altogether wise when it led you to wear your second-best overcoat to the funeral of a second-rate fellow; in the tenacious way his mind clung to the tough belief that life to be good must be hard; that life was work, not play; that the simpler virtues brought the rounded good. Local traditions and responsibilities had their value. Yankee judgment, sound judgment, was a good base, if you could leaven it with an occasional unreasoned enthusiasm. You could be considerate and reasonable and kind if now and then you burned with a passion that was beyond these, and drew on the stars. Take your share of work, and do not count the costs. Good sense, with a humanitarian turn, would keep you from becoming overtechnical. Reach an exact issue and avoid generalities, which are tempting but illusive.

The sense of loneliness runs through all of Holmes' thought. I do not believe it can be attributed solely to what he felt was the inevitable single path of original thinking.

Only when you have worked alone,—[he said to the Harvard undergraduates four years after he had become a judge] when you have felt around you a black gulf of solitude more isolating than that which surrounds the dying man, and in hope and in despair have trusted to your own unshaken will,—then only will you have achieved. Thus only can you gain the secret isolated joy of the thinker, who knows that, a hundred years after he is dead and forgotten, men who never heard of him will be moving to the measure of his thought,—the subtile rapture of a postponed power, which the world knows not because it has no external trappings, but which to his prophetic vision is more real than that which commands an army.

This sense of loneliness was fed during the period when he was writing these words from a half-veiled knowledge that the men around him did not appreciate what he was doing, and that his work was better than its reception suggested. When he left Boston and found so easily his stride in a more sympathetic surrounding, this sense of unappreciated effort is eased; except when, now and again, the feeling of a static and stubborn opposition on his Court evokes it. When Brandeis joined the Court, the feeling of relief to have some one else share the fight and human direction of his views must have grown about him as a warm comfort. As he grew older, and the young secretaries came to Washington so eagerly each year, and went away, his instinct of fatherhood may have stirred uneasily, for he had no son. His irony, which had become gentler though no less apposite, would lead him to say to us:

You see, my boy, with my secretaries I have all the pleasures of parenthood, without any of the responsibilities. If there is anything there, perhaps I can enrich it, and you will go away not altogether ungrateful. If not, no harm is done. . .

VI

Like all men, Holmes tended to generalize from his own spiritual experience. His direction as a young man had been clear; his work in the special field of legal history and criticism had pushed deep roots and had flowered splendidly when he was still comparatively young. Remembering this early success, he said, twenty years later, in an introduction to a reprint of Montesquieu's *Esprit des Lois:*

It often is said, and with a good deal of truth, that men reach their highest mark between thirty and forty . . . men generally have settled down to their permanent occupation by thirty, and in the course of the next ten years are likely to have found such leading and dominant conceptions as they are going to find; the rest of life is working out details.

Holmes at least had found his dominant conceptions before he was forty and never thereafter saw any reason to change them.

Holmes was, like Montesquieu, in the great tradition of the eighteenth-century men of the world, their roots reaching into the century before, when men were content to be universal, their personalities and scope unlimited by their callings, which were incidental. Montesquieu, too, was a judge, and had written a great book on law, a book which, like *The Common Law*, was based on his observations of life, and illumined by his intuitions. His profession had not maimed his personality. He was not, like so many of his contemporaries, a preacher, pamphleteer, publicist; but throughout his life remained the skeptical and amused observer who refused to become a professional man. Holmes felt drawn to this kindred spirit who, rather than write a treatise on the psychology of women, could observe that: *Tous les maris sont laids.*

Holmes had come of age in a generation whose thinking was profoundly disturbed by the new teaching of John Stuart Mill, Darwin and Huxley. He was absorbed in Mill's writings, as his father had indicated to Motley when Wendell went to England at the age of twenty-five. The next fifteen years found him deep in law—practicing, speculating, writing, lecturing—and he left economics alone. It is not far from the mark to conclude that his thinking in the field of economics stopped at

twenty-five. The subject bored him. The conclu-
sions of the professors and the reformers, the pro-
gressives, as they later called themselves, had the
smell of searching for magic which characterized
the philosophers, particularly William James, without any of their charm. The whole field seemed to
bristle with lumpy facts which could not be tested
to find their significance or their trend. Unlike
Brandeis, he had no desire to shape economic forces
under the application of his will, wished to build no
new world about him, and was profoundly skeptical about the ability of these eager young men to do
so. One of the many contradictions of his personality was his fastidious disrelish for facts as such,
coupled with a corresponding distrust of generalities.

"I never know any facts about anything," he told
Pollock, "and always am gravelled when your
countrymen ask some informal intelligent question
about our institutions or the state of politics or
anything else. My intellectual furniture consists of
an assortment of general propositions which grow
fewer and more general as I grow older." That he
didn't read the newspapers was not an affectation,
but because information bored him, although he

liked odd rarities when they pointed to an idea. Facts, after all, he used to say, were useful only to illustrate the perfection of a philosophic conclusion, just as a string of pearls might emphasize the beauty of a lovely neck and shoulders.

Doubtless if he had pursued his economic studies as he went deeper into law he would not have been left for the rest of his life with the set of oversimplified economic assumptions which at times make his expressions sound naïve and not always unprejudiced. For a man who was so skeptical about philosophic systems he was curiously uncritical about the orthodox economic axioms on which he had been brought up. The new ideas had come, of course, with the impact of a revolutionary movement on his generation, and had done much to free it from the gloomy inevitability and dogma of the inherited Puritan Calvinism of the day. Individualism, the play of free trade and free thought, *laissez faire*—these concepts dominated American thought after the Civil War and during the Reconstruction period even up to the Great War, and had not lost their influence during the hard days that came after. It is interesting that Holmes should have so completely accepted their implications and allowed them to color his own beliefs, yet should not have permitted his preferences to grow into the religious atmosphere which, among other men, raised these principles above the plane on which they could be discussed.

Commenting on his constitutional opinions, Mr. Justice Frankfurter, then at the Harvard Law School, has noted this freedom of Holmes from any insistence that his moral axioms should be applied to others. "What makes these opinions significant," Frankfurter writes, "beyond their immediate expression is that they come from a man who, as a judge, enforces statutes based upon economic theories which he does not share, and of whose efficacy in action he is sceptical." Perhaps this is not so surprising, except that it is so rare, when we consider that liberalism as a culture springs from a way of living, and that it is natural that one who accepts a free exchange in the market place should permit it also in the arena of thought.

Yet where no constitutional question was involved, he did not hesitate to give expression to his own economic views in opinions as well as speeches. One of the theories he held most dear, perhaps because he imagined it had been his particular discovery, which we find running through his thought for fifty years, is that much reform is based on the fallacy of thinking in terms of ownership instead of in terms of consumption. The real problem, he believed, is not who owns but who consumes the stream of goods. In *Plant* v. *Woods* the Massachusetts Supreme Court sustained an injunction against the members of a labor union restraining threatened strikes and boycotts to force their employers to make non-members join the union. Holmes dissented. The purpose of the defendants to strengthen their union he believed justified. But he did not want to be thought approving strikes, about which he cherished no illusions.

I think it pure phantasy to suppose that there is a body of capital of which labor as a whole secures a larger share by that means. The annual product, subject to an infinitesimal deduction for the luxuries of the few, is directed to consumption by the multitude, and is consumed by the multitude, always . . . It is only by divesting our minds of questions of ownership and other machinery of distribution, and by looking solely at the question of consumption,—asking ourselves what is the annual product, who consumes it, and what changes would or could we make,—that we can keep in the world of realities.

Plant v. *Woods* was decided in 1900. Six years later we find him writing to Pollock: "My hobby is to consider the stream of products, to omit all talk about ownership and just to consider who eats the wheat, wears the clothes, uses the railroads and lives in the houses. I think the crowd now has substantially all there is, that the luxuries of the few are a drop in the bucket, and that unless you make war on moderate comfort there is no general economic question." This theme continually runs through his thinking. "Most people reason dramatically not quantitatively," he reminds Pollock in 1912, "and never ask how much is withdrawn from the total by the palaces and dinners at Sherry's. I am told that 85 per cent of the annual product here and in England is consumed by people with not over 1,000 dollars a year . . . the crowd has substantially all there is." He constantly recurred to this belief in talk, confirming it by examples from his own experience, such as the impossibility, as he once told me, of finding a designer for a piece of jewelry; the best designers were working for the multitude who bought paste at the five and tens.

He would lash out, quite unexpectedly sometimes, at the contemporary efforts to alleviate suffering, or modify environment. There was enough of the Puritan in him to make him assume a place for suffering in our world. He mildly resented the futile attempt to change the natural order of things. At times he sounds a little petulant, a little as if he were repeating the chamber of commerce commonplaces of the time so dear to other American hearts. And these commonplaces were not confined to the earlier days in Massachusetts but find their way into the Washington scene. There is an impatience about them, as if this grubby activity of the reformers tended to flatten the gallant adventure of the world. In 1895 he said to the graduating class at Harvard:

Meantime we have learned the doctrine that evil means pain, and the revolt against pain in all its forms has grown more and more marked. From societies for the prevention of cruelty to animals up to socialism, we express in numberless ways the notion that suffering is a wrong which can be and ought to be prevented, and a whole literature of sympathy has sprung into being which points out in story and in verse how hard it is to be wounded in the battle of life, how terrible, how unjust it is that any one should fail.

Later, attacks on the court seemed to him to spring from the new unrest that rebelled against law and order and found expression in these half-baked reforms. "When the ignorant are taught to doubt," he said in a speech in 1913, "they do not know what they safely may believe. And it seems to me that at this time we need education in the obvious more than investigation of the obscure. I do not see so much immediate use in committees on the high cost of living and inquiries how far it is due to the increased production of gold, how far to the narrowing of cattle ranges and the growth of population, how far to the bugaboo, as I do in bringing home to people a few social and economic truths." This seems an extraordinary outburst from the old skeptic whose teaching had been that "to have doubted one's own first principles is the mark of a civilized man," and had asserted the duty of inquiry into the play of social needs. Some trace of the irritated moralist, deep within, whose formulated economic outlook had been jarred by the current trends, must have risen to the surface. The present time—1923 when he wrote—seemed to him to be experimenting in negations—"an amusing sport if it is remembered that while it takes but a few minutes to cut down a tree it takes a century for a tree to grow." He did not change his mind that Malthus was right "in fundamental notion," even if the rise of the birth rate was decreasing in America and had become stationary in France, perhaps from some unearthed biologic reason which asserted itself even in the absence of pestilence and war. Malthus is as far as we've got, he thought, or are likely to get. Malthus ran a rapier through the vitals of these humbugs a hundred years ago, yet they are still alive today as optimists who are prophesying the millennium, saying that this or that selfishness will disappear. But surely "my neighbor is better nourished by eating his own dinner than by my eating it for him . . . Men believe what they want to. . . But reason means truth and those who are not governed by it take the chances that some day the sunken fact will rip the bottom out of their boat." A lot of this humbug, he thought, had to do with this modern passion for equality, which motivated his friend, Harold Laski. It was all right when you were a lad, and as a youth he had been an Abolitionist, and had shuddered at a Negro minstrel show, as belittling a suffering race. But you cannot have wholesale regeneration without conscious, co-ordinated effort. Tinkering with the institution of property won't help.

94

Again we see a contradiction in his nature, the dualism of skeptic and moralist, of doubter and preacher; he distrusted affirmations; yet, and not less as his experience broadened, made them with an oversimplification that was only partially concealed by the form of witty aphorism which they usually took. But the contradictions never disturbed the strength or wholeness of his character and maturity; it was as if, like his vast stretches of work and of reading, they too fell into place and obeyed the command of his conscious will.

Holmes wrote while on the Massachusetts bench, as Associate Justice for seventeen years and as Chief Justice for three years, about thirteen hundred opinions. His few economic axioms, at which I have hinted, his skepticism, his sense of a fluid industrial society that cannot be cloaked in a strait jacket of revealed law, will not change when he goes to Washington. But his insight grows as the scene expands; his style becomes terser, more inevitable; there is a broader sense of humanity. The immortal opinions, with their wisdom, and sweep, and poetry will flow from the national background. Yet the Massachusetts opinions are rich at their roots with the fertilization of his informed curiosity and the breadth of his approach to constitutional construction. The House of Representatives asks the opinion of the justices as to whether the legislature can enact woman suffrage with a proviso that the act, if rejected by the people, shall not go into effect. He cannot agree with his brethren that anything in the state constitution, expressly or by implication, forbids such a procedure. "I think that in construing the Constitution," he writes, "we should remember that it is a frame of government for men of opposite opinions and for the future, and therefore not hastily import into it our own views, or unexpressed limitations derived merely from the practice of the past."

His irony is remorseless but accurate, touching rather unpromising facts into sudden incandescence. In a case in which the mayor of New Bedford was sued for firing a policeman, Holmes remarks dryly: "The petitioner may have a constitutional right to talk politics, but he has no constitutional right to be a policeman." He suggests that "if it is a bad rule, that is no reason for making a bad exception to it"; concludes that "a boy who is dull at fifteen probably was dull at fourteen;" points out that "a

horse car cannot be handled like a rapier." In a case
dealing with the responsibility of an owner of a
horse for damage from a kick, he remarks: "It used
to be said in England, under the rule requiring
notice of the habits of an animal, that every dog
was entitled to one worry, but it is not universally
true that every horse is entitled to one kick." With
a polite but none the less satisfying irony, he writes:
"If a single woman not otherwise distinguished
should be minded to prolong the remembrance of
her family name by a beautiful monument over her
grave, we could not pronounce it unsuitable or im-
proper as matter of law."

His distrust for maxims and phrases plants warn-
ings to beware of an easy acceptance of formulas
worn smooth by repetition.

General maxims are oftener an excuse for the want
of accurate analysis than a help in determining the
extent of a duty or the construction of a statute.

The greatest danger . . . is that of being misled by
ready-made generalizations, and of thinking only in
phrases to which as lawyers the judges have become
accustomed, instead of looking straight at things and
regarding the facts in all their concreteness as a jury
would do.

The Bar Association of Boston gave the Chief Justice a dinner, the day before his birthday, two years before he was to leave them. He was fifty-nine, and must have had the sense of slipping time—there was so much to achieve—that led him to write Pollock, two years before, "I turned 57 the other day, but still feel the spring." (It may be doubted whether Pollock ever felt the spring. . .) To the bar Holmes said, a little youthfully, still with that passionate eagerness to conquer and to achieve:

I look into my book in which I keep a docket of the decisions of the full court which fall to me to write, and find about a thousand cases. A thousand cases, many of them upon trifling or transitory matters, to represent nearly half a lifetime! A thousand cases, when one would have liked to study to the bottom and to say his say on every question which the law ever has presented, and then to go on and invent new problems which should be the test of doctrine, and then to generalize it all and write it in continuous, logical, philosophic exposition, setting forth the whole corpus with its roots in history and its justifications of expedience real or supposed!

And he tried to formulate his philosophy of life to them:

We cannot live our dreams. . . The joy of life is to put out one's power in some natural and useful or harmless way. . . The rule of joy and the law of duty seem to me all one . . . the end of life is life. Life is action, the use of one's powers. . . Life is an end in itself, and the only question as to whether it is worth living is whether you have enough of it. . .

The speech disappointed William James. O. W. H. seemed "unable to make any other than that one set speech which comes out on every occasion," he wrote a friend. It was all right for once to celebrate more vital excitement, *joie de vivre*. But to make it systematic, oppose it to the other duties, was to pervert it—"especially when one is a Chief Justice." It was childish, and reminded James of Browning's verse, which Santayana said Attila or Alaric might have written: "Bound dizzily to the wheel of Change, to slake the thirst of God." Mere excitement was an immature ideal, "unworthy of the Supreme Court's official endorsement."

VII

He wrote in the black book, "July 25, [1902] Presdt. offered me Judgeship."

He was sixty-one. He was pretty comfortable in the pleasant routine of his life in Boston. He was the Chief in his own State; and would be only a "side-judge" in Washington. He doubted if Fanny would like the change. But she urged him to accept, saying that they had never appreciated him in Boston. A greater world was opening. There could really be no question of his choice.

On August 13 he confided to Pollock, telling him the news, "Some at least of the money powers think me dangerous, wherein they are wrong." He knew himself, knew his points of view, prejudices if you like. He was not one who would tinker with the institution of property. But he would open the door to thought, and use his strength to hold it open, for many years to come, an exercise the significance of which neither the new judge nor the money powers suspected.

Mrs. Wister, to whom, from time to time he had sent copies of his speeches—"The Use of Colleges" in 1891, "The Soldier's Faith" in 1895—laying them at her feet, as he was pleased to tell her, for they were still living in the nineties, longing, when he sent them, for those delicious notes in the fine, thin hand, which invariably found the words of encouragement out of the great world she represented of which Boston was but a dry and distant echo—Mrs. Wister wrote one of the most charming letters he had ever received, and he answered her fervidly: "You know how to say the things that sting one with joy." And then, as if to mute the expression, to bring it back to earth: "I am glad that our felicitations may be mutual in view of Owen's brilliant success, becoming every day more assured."

The complete lack of understanding of the newspaper reaction to his appointment vexed him, although he knew that on the whole the nomination had been well received. An editorial in the *New York Post* suggested that he had been more of a "literary feller" than one often finds on the bench, and had a strong tendency to be "brilliant" rather than sound. Doubtless *The Post* felt it was unsound to be brilliant, although it might not necessarily follow that to be dull was always to be sound. No one had accused his predecessor, Justice Horace Gray, of being brilliant. He combined an enveloping memory with great learning, but somehow lacked spark, did not have the "instinct for the jugular," that Choate had attributed to John Quincy Adams. Holmes used to say of Gray that the premise of his opinion and the conclusion stood forth like precipices, with a roaring torrent of precedents between, but he never quite understood how Gray got across . . .

The notices in the papers, Holmes wrote Pollock, made him want to vent his rage, at least his dissatisfaction. There was no personal discrimination, no courage, and even their praise had "the flabbiness of American ignorance." It was the same when his book had come out, they had to wait for England to speak. They knew only that he had taken the "labor side" in *Vegelahn* v. *Guntner* six years before, and as the decision had frightened some money interests they suggested that he had partial views, was not sound. And this after he had broken his heart trying to make every word living and real. His deepest wish and the passion of his soul had been to make clear what the aims of the law were or should be, using history, economics, and philosophy to that end. The duffers didn't know anything about it. He felt alone in a desert now that his moment of triumph had come. He had dissented from a view which held picketing "an unlawful interference with the rights both of employer and of employed"; and Mr. Justice Allen had even intimated that, beyond threats of violence, "there also may be a moral intimidation which is illegal." Holmes had seen the necessity of combinations of labor to meet the combinations of capital. Free competition, which is but an expression of the struggle for life, demanded combination. This was a fundamental axiom of society, a very condition of life, against which it was futile to set our faces. And to the undiscriminating world it followed that he had taken the side of labor. Of course he knew that the true grounds of his decision—as of the majority for that matter—had been considerations of policy and social advantage, not merely general propositions of law, which nobody disputes, that is nobody who counted.

He couldn't help letting out an "ebullition of spleen" to Pollock. . . But to the men who counted, after all, it was not the sound of the mob that told, but the expression of their peers. It was "not place or power or popularity" that made "the success that one desires, but the trembling hope that one has come near to an ideal. The only ground that warrants a man for thinking that he is not living the fool's paradise if he ventures such a hope is the voice of a few masters. . ."

The spleen didn't last. The Chicago Bar gave him a banquet on October 20, on the occasion of his address at the dedication of the Northwestern University Law School building, at the invitation of his friend Wigmore, and he "was a howling swell for a time." They liked the speech. After all the next pleasantest thing to being intelligently cracked up oneself was to give a boost to a younger man who deserves it, and Wigmore did. He felt it his duty, Holmes told his audience, to recognize the unadvertised first-rate that was in Wigmore, his learning and originality and the delicacy of his production, which deserved more public recognition. His teaching would satisfy men's need for knowledge, but also would "send them forth with a pennon as well as with a sword, to keep before their eyes in the long battle the little flutter that means

ideals, honor, yes, even romance, in all the dull
details."

He had to be generous to Wigmore to wipe out
that smart of the papers being ungenerous to him;
and because the young fellow had pretty generally
pitched into him.

Holmes' appointment as a justice of the United
States Supreme Court was confirmed on December
4. The new justice moved to Washington on December 6, and was sworn in December 8. Owen
Wister sent him a "dear" telegram which arrived
just before he left the New Willard for the Court,
and Holmes wrote him: "Egotism vanishes in the
great business to be done. I hope I may do my share
nobly, but It not I is the thing one thinks of."

In its January issue *The Green Bag* ("An Enter-
taining Magazine for Lawyers") essayed an ap-
praisal of the new justice. A photograph portrays
him in the typical Prince Albert of the period, with
the long, drooping mustaches, lean and erect, the
mass of hair not yet white, the eyes not as piercing
as in the later pictures. The article suggests that he
had a desire to reduce law to a principle of science,
so far as possible, at least in his own mind. He
thought it proper to regard law as a great "anthro-

A picture of Mr. Justice Holmes about the time he was appointed to
the United States Supreme Court

pological document," to discover what ideals of
society have been strong enough to reach that final
form of expression. It embodied, he had said, the
history of civilization, the moral history of the race
in rules of law. It sank to formalism unless it grew,
thriving on but few rules over a series of successive
approximations. . . A trait of the new justice
was considered his unwillingness to admit restric-
tions upon the powers of the lawmaking or administrative department of the Government not plainly
contained in some specific portion of the Constitution.

Holmes counted on about ten years of active
service. Only two of his associates were younger,
McKenna and White, whose service in the Civil
War was a bond with the Massachusetts man, who
had fought on the other side. White chewed tobacco, but he was hardly an orthodox chewer. He
would send out a page boy to buy a few five-cent
cigars, break them in pieces, and put a piece in his
mouth, and the others in his pockets. When he was
made Chief Justice, he gave up the habit as a little
undignified for the Chief. John Marshall Harlan
also chewed, and Holmes liked to refer to him as

the last of the tobacco-spitting judges. When Harlan was bored with the argument, or restless, he formed a habit of getting up and striding up and down behind his brethren, his hands in the ample pockets of his business cutaway, stopping for an instant at one end of the platform, where the clerk sat in front of a spittoon, or at the other, where the marshal was similarly seated. Holmes watched him with a twinkling deferential admiration. A great fellow, thought Holmes, who admired low tastes but hardly practiced them. He had tried chewing on lonely sentry duty during the war, but had never managed to achieve the habit. It was too much for him. He remembered how his uncle, John Holmes, had to smoke five-cent cigars for fear that his taste would become too refined. Chewing tobacco was better than Moody's practice of keeping a box of hard candy by his elbow and eating from it all day, with a sort of methodical persistence. . .

George Shiras of Pennsylvania, who was seventy, resigned the next year almost as soon as he was entitled to his pension, but continued to live inconspicuously to ninety-two. The Chief Justice, Melville Weston Fuller, was in point of age next to Shiras, and a few months older than Harlan, who outlived him by one year. Holmes grew to have a genuine affection for Fuller, who had been at the Harvard Law School ten years before himself. There was something mellow and benign about him, with the long white locks, almost touching his shoulders, and the immense mustaches. He would put a cigar in his mouth as soon as he left the bench, and a page boy lighted it, terrified lest he singe the august whiskers and set the great man on fire. The page boys adored him, for he would give them each a shiny new five-dollar gold piece on Christmas Day. . . Holmes formed the habit of dropping in to see the Chief on Sunday afternoons at the vast rambling Victorian brick house on the northwest corner of 18th and F Streets.

White had a way of becoming excited over the political consequences of his decisions, which to Holmes so often sounded like stump speeches, with their superfluous long-windedness, a default of the quality of his broad, instinctive statesmanship. But Fuller didn't give a whoop about politics, or what the public thought, or anything else, once his mind was made up, and would not be paragraphed out of his place, as he liked to say to Holmes. What impressed Holmes with the Chief was his administra-

tive side. Holmes, conscious of his own distaste
for anything that approached administrative detail, the handling of affairs, greatly admired it in
others. It seemed wonderful to him that Fuller
could turn off the matters that daily call for action
easily, swiftly, with the least possible friction, with
imperturbable good humor. . . When Fuller died
in 1910, Holmes wrote to his friend, Judge William
LeBaron Putnam of the First Circuit, that the
funeral services at Sorrento had moved him through
and through. Everything conspired with the natural
feeling of the moment.

The coffin, spread with a coverlet of flowers, was
put on a buckboard to go from the house to the
church; the birds were singing; the clergyman, a fine
fellow whom I daresay you know, read extremely
well; a little choir of four young men sang touchingly.

When Chief Justice Taft was sick for a few
weeks, Holmes had to act as Chief, and take over
the detail administration of the Court, which he
thoroughly disliked. Mr. Charles Elmore Cropley,
the clerk of the Court, bringing some orders for him
to sign at his house at 1720 I Street, waited for an
hour before the Justice came down to his library.
"Your eminence," he said to the young man, "I am

not an early bird—and besides, I don't give a damn for worms."

Holmes never could understand Harlan, who seemed to him to be discoursing continually about the rights of the people, a demagogue rather than a thinker. His opinions were interminably long and he never caught the ultimate, which slipped through his powerful vise, the jaws of which couldn't be got nearer than two inches to each other. Harlan seemed hard and humorless. But one day, the day that Holmes was seventy, there was a little nosegay of violets before him on the bench; and he discovered it was from Harlan, and was moved, and it stirred him to find a hidden spring of tenderness in the older man, who after all had fought the battle according to his lights. . .

The old Supreme Court room stood on the main floor of the Capitol, slightly north of the Rotunda, between the Senate and the House, integrated with each, with no aloofness of lonely splendor. There the Senate had sat from 1800 to 1859; and the same room had heard Webster and Calhoun and Clay, the Hayes-Tilden contest, the legal tender cases, and was to hear the great dissents in the *Abrams* and *Schwimmer* cases. "The room," wrote the editor of the American Bar Association Journal recently, "with its columns of native Potomac marble, painted grayish walls, mahogany furnishings and background of red drapes and carpets, presents a picture of such simplicity in contrast to the new Court Chamber, that the impression is one of a drawing room rather than a hall of justice." The robing room was opposite the Court, on the west side. The justices passed from the robing room across the Capitol corridor to the Court Room, led by the venerable Chief Justice Fuller, through the spectators held back by silk ropes between which the justices strode. And once, as he liked to remember, Holmes heard a countryman say to his wife, in awed tones: "Christ, what dignity!" On the floor below, not far from the Senate barber shop, was the conference room, between a little anteroom and a room where they lunched on conference days. Here had once been the old Congressional library, before the Capitol had been burned in 1814. The Supreme Court had no library of its own; but there was a Congressional law library across the hall. None of the justices had offices at that time. Later Mr. Justice Sutherland was allotted chambers on the gallery floor. Mr. Justice Sanford had a space walled off to use as an office, which was later inherited by Mr. Justice Roberts.

The four page boys sat on a leather sofa during conference, and brought water or cigars, or cashed checks and ran errands, while the deliberations took place, which, as Holmes liked to say, would occasionally descend to the vernacular. But, in 1909, the *Knoxville Water Co.* case was decided. Old Albert H. Walker, who wore buckled shoes and looked like Longfellow, was always in Court and knew that the decision would control the *Consolidated Gas* case, which would soon follow. He walked out of Court and bought heavily of Consolidated Gas, and in a few hours the Consolidated Gas opinion justified his judgment; there was talk of a leak and great excitement; and thereafter the page boys were excluded from the conferences.

A year before Holmes' appointment, President Theodore Roosevelt had directed his Attorney General, Philander C. Knox of Pennsylvania, to sue for the dissolution of the Northern Securities Company as a combination in restraint of trade under the Sherman Antitrust Act. The Northern

Securities was a holding company organized by
J. P. Morgan and James J. Hill to consolidate the
Northern Pacific, the Great Northern and the Chicago, Burlington and Quincy railroads. The suit
initiated the President's new trust-busting policy
against the "malefactors of great wealth." There
had been a near panic in Wall Street over the mere
institution of the action, and the President, sniffing
battle, looked around for a justice who would be
on his side of the controversy, to fill Gray's place.
He had no illusions that judges were merely um-
pires. They not only modified but created great
policies. They must be, he said at a dinner in honor
of Harlan in 1902, not only great jurists but also
great statesmen. He knew Harlan would be all
right. Holmes had seemed to be on the side of labor
up in Massachusetts, and therefore presumably
against capital, to make a simplification, a process
which Mr. Roosevelt never found inconvenient.
Holmes' "labor decisions which have been criti-
cized," he wrote Henry Cabot Lodge, "by some of
the big railroad men and other members of large
corporations constitute to my mind a strong point
in [his] favor. . . Finally, Judge Holmes' whole
mental attitude . . . is such that I should naturally

expect him to be in favor of those principles in which I so earnestly believe."

But the President wasn't sure. On the centennial of the day on which Marshall took his seat as Chief Justice, February 4, 1901, Holmes had made an address about Marshall which seemed to the President unworthy. "If I were to think of John Marshall simply by number and measure in the abstract," the judge had said, "I might hesitate in my superlatives. . ." This doubtless was the basis of the President's hesitation, although Holmes had hastened to add:

But such thinking is empty in the same proportion that it is abstract. It is most idle to take a man apart from the circumstances which, in fact, were his. . . A great man represents a great ganglion in the nerves of society, or, to vary the figure, a strategic point in the campaign of history, and part of his greatness consists of his being *there*.

This kind of talk smacked of heresy to the robust Republican President. Surely a man was not fitted for this exalted position unless in the "higher sense" he was a party man, and co-operated with his fellow statesmen in the other branches of the government, like Washington and Marshall and

Adams—not like Taney, who was "a curse to our national life because he belonged to the wrong party and faithfully carried out the criminal and foolish views of the party. . ." It was true, he added, writing to Lodge, that "the majority of the present Court . . . have, although without satisfactory unanimity, upheld the policies of President McKinley and the Republican party in Congress," thus rendering a great service to mankind. He wanted to know that Holmes "was in entire sympathy with our views . . . was . . . absolutely sane and sound on the great national policies. . ."

It is a little surprising that Roosevelt appointed Holmes.

And a year later, when the *Northern Securities* case was decided in favor of the Government, Holmes dissented, leading with him Chief Justice Fuller, White, and Peckham. He was not upholding the principles of President McKinley or faithfully carrying out the beliefs of the Great Republican Party—or, incidentally, of the President.

Roosevelt was furious. He did not hesitate to say that he would never have appointed Holmes if he had known that Holmes would decide against him.

The President had evidently forgotten that he had said to Senator Lodge that he had found in Holmes a judge who was able to preserve the aloofness of his mind. The President even thought of excluding the Justice from the White House, but was dissuaded. The Justice remembered that the President had once remarked that a nation could never be great while it was governed by lawyers, clerks, and women, and recalled that a Senator had once said about him: "What the boys like about Roosevelt is that he doesn't care a damn for the law." The truth was that he could never forgive any one who stood in his way. The episode broke an incipient friendship, which was not restored when the President some time later wrote to Holmes that he had just finished reading his "Speeches," and that they were the finest since Lincoln.

Holmes didn't tell Roosevelt that he despised the Sherman Act. It was hardly the time or place. But he told others when he felt like it. The theory of the act was that you must compete but you mustn't win the competition. Of course he upheld any constitutional laws Congress saw fit to pass. But this law was humbug based on ignorance and incompetence, an absurd statute. And the Interstate Commerce Commission was always trying to extend its power.

Soon after Roosevelt died, Holmes wrote Pollock:

He was very likeable, a big figure, a rather ordinary intellect, with extraordinary gifts, a shrewd and I think pretty unscrupulous politician. He played all his cards —if not more. *R. i. p.*

VIII

WHEN Holmes took his seat in the Court it was 112 years old, and he was to sit for nearly 30 years. Between Marshall, who was commissioned in 1801, and Fuller, there had been but three Chief Justices. Three more were to follow Fuller while Holmes was on the bench. Fifteen associate justices were appointed while he sat. When he retired he had participated in more than a third of the Court's decisions.

During these years profound changes had been going on in American society. Wealth was shifting from individual direct ownership of tangible assets to the more fluid but less responsible ownership of corporate securities, bringing about a change in the relation of employer and workmen, greatly complicated by the problem of absentee ownership. The frontiers had been reached, free land no longer could absorb migration, the shift from an agricultural to an urban civilization continued, and men began somewhat cautiously to think in terms of security and conservation rather than wholly in the symbols of exploitation. Yet the psychology of the pioneer had not disappeared with the loss of his horizon; and the frontier mind, strengthened in judicial expression by the moral concepts which hovered like a halo over the cruder realities, unable to conform to the new pressures of a different world, resisted change with a vigorous tenacity that lasted for the years that Holmes sat on the Court. The automobile was being introduced when Holmes came to Washington; when he resigned air travel was competing with passenger trains. The power age followed the machine age; mass production glutted the markets; labor had learned to combine, became strong. The concentration of wealth in a few corporations, in a tiny fraction of the population, increased. Finally came the first World War, the consequent extraordinary technological improvement, the paralyzing depression, chronic unemployment.

The problems before the Court covered a broad field, and were of intense political and public interest to the country, trying to readjust itself in order to live under the changed conditions. The relation of government to business was of increasing importance, fought over against a background of vigorous disagreement. Under every administration the powers of the national government increased, new control and regulatory bodies were set up; and men who looked on this development as an impertinent invasion of individual rights turned to the courts for protection. Lawyers, who had always been dominant in molding American public institutions, distrusted and resisted the growth of administrative agencies, and their successful functioning that cut across the pleasant field of *laissez faire*, with results that disregarded the boundaries that separated judicial and executive, legislative and judicial, prosecution and tribunal. The bar fought this encroachment on what they considered the proper function of the courts, as, a hundred years before, they had resisted the equitable procedures introduced to modify the rigidities of law courts. Social regulation, to those who wanted to be let alone, became synonymous with tyranny, and socialism became a war cry in their mouths. The Federal Government and the states must be checked in the courts. Men's material ambitions found expression in moral shibboleths.

Of these Professor Edward S. Corwin, in his

Twilight of the Supreme Court, gives two or three fervid examples. He recalls Mr. Joseph Choate's argument to the Supreme Court condemning the income tax of 1894 as "communistic in its purposes and tendencies . . . defended here upon principles as communistic, socialistic—what shall I call them [how ineffectual were the old words to express the horror of the tax!]—populistic as ever have been addressed to any political assembly in the world."

The year before he was appointed to the Supreme Court, George Sutherland, then a United States Senator from Utah, had expressed his views in broad moral terms:

There is nothing more unfortunate in governmental administration [he said] than a policy of playing fast and loose with great economic and political principles which have . . . become part of our fundamental wisdom . . . Conditions . . . may change . . . but the principle itself is immutable; once righteous, it is always righteous. . . There are certain fundamental social and economic laws which are beyond the power, and certain underlying governmental principles, which are beyond the right of official control, and any attempt to interfere with their operation inevitably ends in confusion, if not disaster.

The outraged moral sanction went beyond history, below the laws and the Constitution, invoking natural rights, which brooked not interference; and we find Mr. John W. Davis asking of the New Deal: "Who can doubt that there are natural laws in the social and economic as well as the physical worlds, and that these cannot be overridden without courting disaster?"

Holmes, with a healthy sense of the strong life of nature, and the slow movement of history, though he had no belief in panaceas, had none in sudden ruin. He distrusted first principles because he knew that judges too often mistook for them the conscious or unconscious sympathies which they read into the law. At the dinner of the Harvard Law School Association of New York he may have been thinking of Choate's argument when he said: "When twenty years ago a vague terror went over the earth and the word socialism began to be heard, I thought and still think that fear was translated into doctrines that had no proper place in the Constitution or the common law;" then added: "Judges are apt to be naïf, simple-minded men, and they need something of Mephistopheles. We too need education in the obvious—to learn to transcend our

own convictions and to leave room for much that
we hold dear to be done away with short of revolution by the orderly change of law."

He knew he himself had something of Mephistopheles.

To understand Holmes' skepticism it is important
to remember the articles of his faith. As Morris
Cohen has pointed out, even if Holmes' mind was
essentially agnostic it was dominated by the Puritan
tradition that insisted on the Calvinistic acceptance
of the daily duty. If he were doubtful of the ultimate values, he had no question about *his* funda-
mentals—health, hard work, courage amid doubt,
an open mind, the will to achieve. Mr. William J.
Kenealy, Dean of the Boston College Law School,
in a recent address, in which he decried the tendency of modern legal pragmatists to speak lightly
of natural law, cited certain remarks of Holmes as
examples of this tendency to reduce morality to
good taste and principles to expediency. He quoted
two vigorous expressions of opinion ("Holmes,"
the dean says, justly enough, "was not a man to
water down his opinions"), one from a letter to
J. C. H. Wu (August 26, 1926), and another in a
letter to Pollock (February 1, 1920):

"I don't believe," Holmes wrote to Wu, "that it is an absolute principle or even a human ultimate that man always is an end in himself—that his dignity must be respected . . . Our morality seems to me only a check on the ultimate domination of force . . ."

And to Pollock, in the same vein: "I think that the sacredness of human life is a purely municipal ideal of no validity outside the jurisdiction. I believe that force, mitigated so far as may be by good manners, is the *ultima ratio* . . ."

Mr. Kenealy pays a compliment to the Justice as "a masterful champion of many just and liberal causes." But that was precisely what Holmes was not—a champion of causes. Yet if he believed no more in principles than in causes, his lack of faith did not interfere with the vigor of his affirmations where his own choice was involved. Holmes' skepticism was primarily rational, and was not imbued with the emotional doubts which, in his generation, had made action so distasteful to Henry Adams, passion so alien to Henry James.

The younger skeptics of the days following the last war, disillusioned certainly by the blank failures which followed the overstimulating promises of the

Fourteen Points, were also bred on the theory of relativity, which undoubtedly the dean had in mind, that might lead them, in the final analysis, to ask whether, after all, *anything* was worth fighting for. But surely they were the spiritual descendants of Adams and of James, not of Holmes, to whom, it cannot be denied, war was glorious—drab and horrible, but glorious in the sense that it represented the ultimate struggle that was life on a plane where sacrifice purged men of the evils of sloth and materialism. To him war had meant manhood, becoming a man, taking his place alongside his father as his father's equal. Anything that you cared passionately enough about was worth fighting for. It was hard for him to think about war impersonally, his war was so much a part of him. It was a simple creed, stemming deep in his Puritan line. Yet it did not compel any ultimate dilemma of the futility of skepticism on one hand or the worship of brutality on the other. If there were contradictions in his own being, they were fused by a belief that extremes need not be reached before a line can be drawn. And if morality was but a check on force, he would none the less spend a life in asserting the value of courage, of truth, of tolerance. Contradictory? Certainly, he would have answered, but so too is life full of contradictions.

Nor did he believe in natural laws, a belief which seemed to him to imply a naïve state of mind that accepted what had been familiar to the believer as something that must be accepted by all men everywhere. Behind the legal rights of man-made rules lurked the emotion of men who to a great extent believed what they wanted to believe. There is no rational ground for being dissatisfied unless our truth is accepted as cosmic truth. Although our experience may make our preferences dogmatic for ourselves we should recognize that others—poor souls—may be equally dogmatic about something else, and may even fight and die to make a world different from the world we should like. Such a view made one tolerant in passing on the beliefs of others.

A year after he had been on the Court he expressed this caution in discussing the power of judges to review legislation, in the particular case a clause in the California constitution prohibiting marginal sales of stock.

While the courts must exercise a judgment of their own, [the opinion ran] it by no means is true that every law is void which may seem to the judges who pass upon it excessive, unsuited to its ostensible end, or based upon conceptions of morality with which they disagree. Considerable latitude must be allowed for differences of view as well as for possible peculiar conditions which this court can know but imperfectly, if at all.

The provisions of the Constitution must be administered with caution and some play allowed for the joints of the machine. They "are not mathematical formulas having their essence in their form; they are organic living institutions transplanted from English soil. Their significance is vital not formal; it is to be gathered not simply by taking the words and a dictionary, but by considering their origin and the line of their growth."

Mr. Justice Frankfurter has noted that to Holmes the Constitution was not primarily a text or dialectic, but a means of ordering the life of a progressive people.

Mr. Justice Holmes [he has written] has recalled us to the traditions of Marshall, that it *is* a Constitution we are expounding, and not a detached document inviting scholastic dialectics. To him the Constitution is a means of ordering the life of a young nation, having its roots in the past—"continuity with the past is not a duty but a necessity"—and intended for the un-known future. Intentionally, therefore, it was bounded with outlines not sharp and contemporary, but permitting of increasing definiteness through experience. . .

In his famous dissent in the *Lochner* case in 1905 to an opinion of the majority striking down a New York law which limited the hours of work in bakeries to ten a day, he urged that the preferences of individual judges should not interfere with the decisions of the legislature. Agreement or disagreement with the objects of legislation is not the point.

The Fourteenth Amendment does not enact Mr. Herbert Spencer's Social Statics. . . Some of these laws embody convictions or prejudices which judges are likely to share. Some may not. But a constitution is not intended to embody a particular economic theory, whether of paternalism and the organic relation of the citizen to the State, or of *laissez faire*. It is made for people of fundamentally differing views, and the accident of our finding certain opinions natural and familiar or novel and even shocking ought not to conclude our judgment upon the question whether statutes embodying them conflict with the Constitution of the United States.

The several states afforded "insulated chambers" where social experiments desired by the community could be made, and the Constitution should not be invoked to prevent the making of these experiments even if they seemed "futile or even noxious to me and to those whose judgment I most respect." He had not forgotten that the prevalent moral and political theories, avowed or unconscious, and the prejudices which judges share with their fellow men, have more to do than syllogism in determining the rules whereby men are governed.

Holmes had suggested on the Massachusetts Court that he had no illusions about the economic value of labor unions. But their members might not unnaturally believe that only by belonging to a union could a fair contract be secured. This view, right or wrong, that liberty of contract begins when equality between the parties had been established, might be held by reasonable men. And he was of the opinion that nothing in the Constitution prevented outlawing "yellow-dog" contracts, which excluded from employment men who joined unions. He might not believe in unions, but Congress might think otherwise, and so pronounce that to foster strong unions was for the best interest not only of the men, but of the railroads. And so might Con-

gress believe that an act prohibiting the shipment in
interstate commerce of goods manufactured from
child labor would improve working standards; and,
exercising its power to regulate interstate commerce, so enact, irrespective of any incidental effect
on state activities.

I should have thought [he wrote in *Hammer* v.
Dagenhart] that if we were to introduce our own
moral conceptions where in my opinion they do not
belong, this was preëminently a case for upholding the
exercise of all its powers by the United States. . .
I had thought that the propriety of the exercise of a
power admitted to exist in some cases was for the
consideration of Congress alone and that this Court
always had disavowed the right to intrude its judgment upon questions of policy or morals. It is not for
this Court to pronounce when prohibition is necessary
to regulation if it ever may be necessary—to say that
it is permissible as against strong drink but not as
against the product of ruined lives.

He knew when these constitutional guaranties
were invoked to prevent the Government from
forbidding certain practices considered unsocial
that men repeated pious generalities to sustain their
prejudices, generalities which constantly grew
softer against the hard facts of a changing in-

dustrial world. So the Fifth Amendment did but in vague contours prohibit the depriving of any person by the Federal Government of liberty or property without due process of law. The same words in the Fourteenth Amendment, applying to the states, were modestly construed at first. "Later that innocuous generality was expanded into the dogma, Liberty of Contract. Contract is not specially mentioned. . . It is merely an example of doing what you want to do, embodied in the word liberty. But pretty much all law consists in forbidding men to do some things that they want to do, and contract is no more exempt from law than other acts." These words were written in dissent from a majority opinion holding unconstitutional a minimum-wage law of the District of Columbia.

IX

It was the spring of 1910. The late afternoon heat dissolved in sudden showers, and the next morning the May sun slowly dried the wet red bricks which reflected the drooping green of sugar maple or lime, that smelled so sweetly. Ladies drove about in little electric broughams, but there were still a few pairs of smartly stepping horses. Mrs. Robert Hinckley drove a pair of grays, and one of them, pawing to shake clear one of these new stops for the traffic, thrust his hoof in an open manhole, while the passing automobiles smiled and waved to the lady sitting very straight in the back of her victoria. . .

Holmes dreamed that he was to be executed, a sort of unpleasant premonition of the approach of *finis*. It made him want to sum up, and he tried—a vain attempt—in a letter to Wister, from whom he had recently had two most welcome letters. It was his eighth term, he wrote, and though to Wister relatively still a youth time might seem longer, to him the years ticked by like seconds.

One's ideals [he said] are different from those of the majority and therefore there is much to discourage. One sees what seems to one second-rate, or no rate, praised and exalted, and one remembers that the majority vote of that nation that can lick all others is the test of truth, and despair would be easy. But there is the escape that it is the majority vote only in the long run, even only in an imaginary long run, and one's own ideals are imperative and the only test for life, for oneself. From that point of view I am happy in a trembling sort of way, and should have liked to have done a great deal more. But I have done as much as I could of what was next to my hand, and I have done it according to my conception of the big way.

This might sound mortuary, but he was good for ten years yet. . . He repeated one of his favorite paradoxes that any book was dead in twenty-five or fifty years. The author's new truths have become familiar, his errors exploded; if an artist, the emotional emphasis has changed. "But for all that a great man is discernible as great. And the great bottom feelings don't change even if the objects of them do." He had been having one great experience —Dante.

I found the intensity of Dante's spiritual rapture so thrilling and absorbing that I could think of little else, and the song of his words is divine. Shakespeare will say a few words now and then that seem the beginning of the road to paradise ("In Belmont lives a Lady," &c.). But Dante does it every 20 lines, and he carries you there too. It is not merely the Italian. When I read the answer to him of the troubadour Arnaut, 'Jeu sui Arnaut, que plor e vau cantan," I had to rush out of doors and walk it off. He weeps for he is still in purgatory, but he is a poet and a troubadour and he goes singing through his tears. Talk about a green thought in a green shade. D's paradise is white on white on white—like a dish of certain tulips in the spring.

But he must have a little room for Rabelais, who had revived him in these later languid days.

What temperament, what gusto. Everything begins to hum—like culture in Chicago. And what a seed book, how many germs of Swift, Sterne, perhaps even Thackeray. You see I am reading now for the Day of Judgment, so as not to dread if I am called up on some book that every gentleman is expected to have read. But I have jawed enough. . . Your aged friend (I shall be 70 at my next birthday!).

He thought a good deal about life that day, for it was his seventieth birthday, and his class at Harvard —what was left of the class of 1861—were to meet at their fiftieth anniversary in June, and he had been asked to speak. He had made no speech since he had come to Washington, had made it a rule to keep his "trap" shut, although of course there had been a good many requests, especially at first. He had been looking through his papers, rearranging them in the evening, while Fanny read aloud, and had run across his brief remarks at Ipswich at the unveiling of the memorial tablets in the summer of 1902. They spoke from a past that seemed shut far behind the Washington days. The brick and shingle of the old Massachusetts towns he had known were dimmer now in remembrance against the well-ordered bustle of Washington. But his philosophy had not changed in the nine years that seemed so much longer, more comprehensive, than all the years on the Massachusetts court. He had said that we all walk by faith. He wondered. Perhaps that was going too far. But the hope that the world might be a little better for our striving was not unworthy of a philosopher. And the very loneliness of self found comfort in the sense of the continuous past that brought the present into a single unity. . . It sounded a little jejune as he read, but not bad on the whole—the "electric example" of those who had gone before; and he read over the last words—"the white sands of Ipswich, terrible as engulfing graves, lovely as the opal flash of fairy walls, will gleam in the horizon, the image of man's mysterious goal."

Henry Bowditch was dead and Frank Emmons. Moorfield Storey was still practicing patent law in Boston, but, Lord, how old he had grown! He walked to the open window and breathed in the dampish air, smelling of buds and earth. He felt again the spring, and for a moment shut his eyes to hold that old poignancy. He walked back to the desk, where the *certiorari* lay heaped in a neat stack, on the top of each case a summary in longhand, by the secretary, of the issues involved. How he hated the *certiorari*. Whenever he won a moment's leisure for reading they would come trooping in with a relentless pressure, all through the year, here and in Beverly. Certioration is the thief of time. Not very good. He'd try it on the secretary tomorrow. He plunged into work. . .

He tried his hand at the speech that night. How had he changed in the fifty years? He wanted to see and feel the forces behind his work, the great social implications beneath the chaotic surface of the cases. That was all that philosophy was, trying to find the unity behind the details, even if there were not unity, and seeing it with an individual eye. The unity was perhaps but the design of the artist in his own brain, and had little to do with those unmanageable facts. He picked up his pen and wrote:

"One learns from time an amiable latitude with regard to beliefs and tastes. Life is painting a picture, not doing a sum. . . Man is born a predestined idealist, for he is born to act." That was it—life was action, and action was affirmation. "To act," he wrote, "is to affirm the worth of an end, and to persist in affirming the worth of an end is to make an ideal. . . Life is a roar of bargain and battle, but in the very heart of it there rises a mystic spiritual tone that gives meaning to the whole. . . It suggests that even while we think that we are egotists we are living to ends outside ourselves."

There was a letter from Oswald Ryan, then a Senior at Harvard, whom he had met, to say how much he had been stirred by Holmes' slim volume of speeches, which Little, Brown and Company had just-republished, and a copy of which the Justice had sent him. Answering, Holmes wrote:

I am glad you got some good out of my speeches, and am much obliged for your telling me so. Life is a romantic business. It is painting a picture, not doing a sum—but you have to make the romance, and it will come to the question how much fire you have in your belly. I wish you good luck in the approaching campaign.

He worked all the next day on his opinion in a case in which he held that West Virginia had to pay for her proportionate share of bonds issued before the old State of Virginia had been split up. A bondholder had written to ask whether he should sell his bonds, "no one seems to know, so I thought I had better write to you as no one else can give me any practical advice. . ."

He should have been warned on that particular April morning by something in Fanny's eye, as she looked across at him at breakfast from behind the kidneys she was stewing for him. He loved stewed kidneys. And the secretary had turned up early when he was still at breakfast, which was a suspicious circumstance in itself, knowing the secretary. Somehow they had inveigled him into making a tour of the house. As a matter of fact, he was apt to go down to the cellar after breakfast to get a worm or two from the worm barrel to take upstairs to feed one of Fanny's birds—the baby starling or the Japanese robin. The baby starling died of excitement a few days later, trying to make a nest, fluttering with bits of paper from the secretary's desk in the front library to the mantelpiece. It grew too excited, and collapsed. They tried giving it a drop of whiskey—it was rather hard to know—but that hadn't done any good. The spring was too much for it, and he felt a twinge of sympathy. . . But on that particular morning they all three went to the cellar, and Fanny was mumbling and muttering something about "cockroaches."

Suddenly the secretary cried: "Come over here, Mr. Justice, I think I see one."

He moved toward the flour barrel. "Nonsense, my lad, no cockroaches would live in a house with Mrs. Holmes."

"But, Mr. Justice, look." Sure enough, large as life, there it was, sitting on the flour in the half-empty barrel.

They all craned.

"Brrr," said Mrs. Holmes, and shivered, "Nasty thing." He looked at her suspiciously. She didn't often shiver. "You grab it," she said to the secretary.

But that young man hesitated.

The Judge pulled back his coat sleeve. "One, two, three!" And he plunged his arm deep in the flour, and brought forth a cockroach, made of wire.

"April fool, old man," said Mrs. Holmes.

He eyed the two conspirators with a deep, long chuckle of enjoyment. And then, to his wife: "You she devil!"

He avoided public dinners, and, after he went to Washington, made only one other address after his remarks at the fiftieth anniversary. In February, 1913, he spoke at a dinner of the Harvard Law School Association of New York. He had been now for ten "accomplished years" on the Court. The Court, he said, like any other institution, had to justify its continuance in life. To be called representatives of a class, the tool of the money power, to receive intimations of corruption, was very painful when one was spending the energies of one's soul trying to do good work. These attacks were but expressions of the unrest that seemed to wonder whether law and order pay. . . He spoke of the need of thinking things instead of words. It is a slow business for our people to reach rational views.

"But as I grow older I grow calm. . . I do not lose my hopes. . . I think it probable that civilization somehow will last as long as I care to look ahead . . ."

He expressed his skepticism of modern panaceas, of the strenuously urged nostrums of the day. But, as always, he also felt the need of affirming his faith, if it could be affirmed but in the mystic form of a trembling dream.

The other day [he ended] my dream was pictured to my mind. It was evening. I was walking homeward on Pennsylvania Avenue near the Treasury, and as I looked beyond Sherman's Statue to the west the sky was aflame with scarlet and crimson from the setting sun. But, like the note of downfall in Wagner's opera, below the sky line there came from little globes the pallid discord of the electric lights. And I thought to myself the Götterdämmerung will end, and from those globes clustered like evil eggs will come the new masters of the sky. It is like the time in which we live. But then I remembered the faith that I partly have expressed, faith in a universe not measured by our fears, a universe that has thought and more than thought inside of it, and as I gazed, after the sunset and above the electric lights there shone the stars.

The same spring he was asked by James A. Lowell to speak at a dinner of the Massachusetts

Bar Association. He must decline, he wrote, but added:

I also might say that I especially wish that I might see the new-comers, because I so sympathize with their anxious interrogation of destiny. Most beginnings I suppose are unhappy. But, through the efforts of Mr. Wigmore and Mr. Pound and some others, the young men of to-day at least are spared the doubt that made my first years wretched—the doubt whether it was possible to reach a philosophic outlook by the pathway of the law and in and through that calling to feed and keep alive the idealizing passion that all of us have in our hearts. That doubt has been laid to rest, but in some form youth is sure to be anxious, and I wish that I could be with you to say "Sursum corda."

A few years later the Harvard Liberal Club asked him to speak at a meeting called to protest against the suppression of free speech when Attorney General A. Mitchell Palmer was conducting his famous raids against the "Reds." For obvious reasons, he wrote, he would not care to speak on such a subject, except as from time to time he had to, and added: "I see no impropriety, however, in suggesting the isolated reflection that with effervescing opinions, as with the not yet forgotten champagnes, the quickest way to let them get flat is to let them get exposed to the air."

Now and then a lawyer who argued a case before them would become a little too smart, sometimes even personal; but he usually stuck out his neck, and you thrust back, not swinging an axe but with the swift plunge of a rapier. So in the *Gavit* case, which James M. Beck as Solicitor General had argued for the Government. The taxpayer had won below in the Second Circuit, which had held that income from a certain trust fund was a gift and therefore not taxable income under the terms of the Revenue Act of 1913. Holmes was interested. He himself enjoyed such an income, and said so during argument by the taxpayer's lawyer, who was too surprised to say anything until the end, when he ventured: "I hope, Mr. Justice Holmes, that the Statute of Limitations will not have run against you, so you will not be foreclosed from getting back the tax you have mistakenly paid out." The others looked at the Judge, who let a long enough moment slip by to allow the slightly self-conscious suspense to point up his reply. "Nothing," said the Justice, "nothing you have said leads me to hope . . ."

He reversed the judgment, dealing with a broad objection in characteristic fashion. "Neither are we troubled by the question where to draw the line. That is the question in pretty much everything worth arguing in the law. *Hudson County Water Co.* v. *McCarter*, 209 U. S., 349, 355. Day and night, youth and age are only types." The *Hudson Water Company* case was one of his own opinions, seventeen years before; *prime* authority, as he said to the secretaries; or if they couldn't find any prime authority, then his opinions in Massachusetts were next best; and last you could cite, if you must cite some precedent, the pronouncements of his living or deceased brethren. A reference at most was enough, quotations usually but padding.

Mr. Beck was an industrious and doubtless learned Philadelphia lawyer, but how long-winded, and how by the yard he loved to quote Shakespeare at them. He belonged, it was understood, to some highly esoteric and venerable Shakespeare society in Philadelphia. The brethren didn't like it, all except perhaps the Chief Justice, Taft in those days, who would go to sleep, very gently, and wake up smiling. Beck liked to end his arguments with a good solid quotation ("not inappropriate," he would suggest); and then, without looking at his brief, he would recite:

> For government, though high, and low, and lower,
> *Put into parts*, doth keep in one concent;
> Congruing in a full and natural close,
> *Like music*.

Or again:

> Can such things be,
> And overcome us like a summer's cloud,
> Without our special wonder?

But finally when Beck declaimed, looking rather angrily at the dozing Chief Justice—

> Force should be right; or, rather, right and wrong,
> (Between whose endless jar justice resides,)
> Should lose their names, and so should justice too.
> Then every thing includes itself in power,
> Power into will, will into appetite;
> And appetite, an universal wolf,
> [Beck seemed to be glowering at the Chief]
> So doubly seconded with will and power,
> Must make perforce an universal prey,
> And, last, eat up himself.

Holmes could stand it no longer, and leaning to the Chief, who sat next to him, whispered in his ear, not inaudibly: "I hope to God Mrs. Beck likes Shakespeare!"

It was nice to hear the Chief, quietly waking, respond with that rich chuckle that did the heart good. . . Beck had the manners of the great world, "but somehow the Philadelphians," Holmes confided to Pollock, were "hopelessly injected with the second rate."

Holmes loved Washington, especially when the spring came, on the very heels of winter, so that often not many weeks elapsed between a late November rose or the jasmine against a sunny January wall, and the first crocuses here and there in the grass that had stayed green, and the bloodroot in Rock Creek Park, and finally the cherry trees. The air of Georgetown in May was full of the smell of box and roses, and what his friend Bob Barlow had called the yelling of birds. He would plunge into his work so that, perhaps for a blessed week, his assignments would be finished, and he could work on the *certiorari* and read his brethren's opinions in the mornings, and take long walks with his secretary in the afternoons. Their opinions he thought almost always too long. They said in pages what should have gone into a sentence or two. They analyzed pleadings, drew on all the facts, when you needed only the salient points of the issue, adorned their talk with the parade of precedent, a pale history of the past that was no part of the immediate need.

One afternoon in late March he had got his secretary out for a long walk along the towpath. It was good to feel as young as he felt at seventy-eight, to enjoy the sound and smell of the spring as he still enjoyed it. The secretary, he considered, as they walked together, looked very smart for a youngster who could have been saving a large part of his salary. Certainly he wasn't worth the $2000 a year— none of these young men were. He hinted that thrift was an admirable virtue; and the young man smiled with such pleasant tolerance that the Justice liked him for the sense of resistance that youth sometimes gives to age, for the suggestion that perhaps extravagance had its points over thrift—which, of course, it hadn't. . . Holmes talked of some of the women he had known. The fun of talking to women, he suggested, was that they carried you away, so that you could express your innards with all the appropriate rapture, floating on the exquisite breath of your own egotism; reaching so far that suddenly you might look at her and say: "By the way, my dear, what is your name?"

They had tea that day with Mrs. Holmes—that is the secretary and Mrs. Holmes; the Judge disliked what he called spoiling his dinner. He was inclined to talk of the Universe, and the secretary to listen. You can't know about it, said the Judge, you can only bet on it, as a varying spontaneity taking an irrational pleasure in moments of apparently rational sequence. So he had termed himself a bettabilitarian. The only cosmic significance of man is that he is part of the cosmos, but that is enough. The great act of faith is to decide that you are not God. Ethics are but a body of imperfect social generalizations expressed in terms of emotion. The truth is but the system of my own limitations. But even if I must leave absolutes to those who are better equipped for handling them, like Josiah Royce, I do not therefore have to sit still and let time run over me. For the mode in which the inevitable comes to pass is through effort. Functioning is all there is, most of it absorbed on the lower levels— victuals, procreation, rest, eternal terror. Cosmically considered, these may not be the lower levels, and an idea no more important than the bowels. One should accept the common lot, with an adequate vitality. . .

The Justice paused. "Talk, Mr. Justice," suggested the secretary, "a little more about your friend the Cosmos."

The Justice stopped, eyeing him with suspicion. "Young man, I know that you are flippant, and I suspect that you are leading me on. . . The Cosmos is everything I don't know, beyond my capacity to predicate, for remember my view that I am in its belly, not the Cosmos in mine. Those philosophic fellows are forever confusing themselves with the universe. Royce cries out 'I am the Absolute!' Then the silence of creation and the scurrying about of many little feet; and finally, from some far-off corner comes a feeble squeak—'Here I am, over in this corner, I the Absolute!' Bradley's Cosmos gets its tail in its mouth, and is as self-supporting as a row of men sitting in each other's laps in a circle. Bertrand Russell rebels against his Cosmos, which is but to damn the weather, evidence of the fellow's ill adjustment. But the systems disappear, and only their insights remain for the unknown multitudes. . . For, after all, the business of philosophy is to show that we are not fools for doing what we want to do."

The Judge looked at the secretary, who smiled.

Mrs. Holmes bit off a thread. She had been sewing. "Pass me the scissors, Wendell," she said.

He got up. "You see," he said to the secretary, "just as I told you, women are all alike. You pour out your heart, your very soul, in the best of talk to them, the whole exciting philosophy of your being. And what do they say—pass me the scissors, Wendell. Do you remember, my boy, the last act of *Man and Superman,* when she's got him, and she throws the feather boa around his neck, and he gathers all his forces in protest, he's lost, his precious freedom is gone; and she smiles, as he talks, she doesn't dispute or argue, she smiles, and when he pauses for breath—'Go on talking, dear,' she says, 'go on talking!'"

He had decided to hear Chaliapin sing next week. The price was beyond reason—five dollars a ticket. It couldn't be worth five dollars to hear Chaliapin. Mrs. Holmes thought that the secretary would like to go.

"He can't afford it," said the Judge.

"I'm afraid not," agreed the secretary.

"We might treat him," suggested Mrs. Holmes.

The Judge eyed the secretary. "I don't think it's worth five dollars," he said.

They discussed it for a moment, but the Judge remained unconvinced.

Before dinner, in the library, he knit his brows over a long opinion of Brandeis, filled with economic data, that Holmes knew nothing about, decorated with concise footnotes referring to trade reports, to studies of committees, to tables of figures. Beautifully clear, though, and on the bull's-eye, thought Holmes, as he leaned back in his chair. He took the opinion, and wrote on the margin:

"This afternoon I was walking on the towpath and saw a cardinal. It seemed to me to be the first sign of Spring. By the way, I concur."

After he had heard Chaliapin sing, the next week, he told the secretary that he had been right—it wasn't worth five dollars.

X

THE WAR had been over for a year. But in the
Court in Washington the remnants of the war
thinking, of the war hysteria, still washed before
the justices the flotsam and jetsam of the war cases.
Holmes felt the anticlimax in dealing with convictions under the war statutes. The trial judges had
lost their heads, he thought, imposing heavy sentences out of all proportion to the criminal acts—
ten, fifteen, twenty years. It was not as if these
wretched little figures had been tried for some
tremendous treason, for passionate and violent protest, staking all and losing all, paying in full for their
revolt against the country where they had been
bred and which was at war, its life in peril. The
country was no longer at war, and he could not
understand why the Government should press these
prosecutions against a few individuals, ill fed, ignorant, darkly disturbed little workmen, maladjusted,
huddled about their wretched little printing presses

in half-deserted houses in Chicago, in Philadelphia, in Boston . . . These men were so anonymous, so unknown, so unimportant—little Socialists, ranting against society, stretching their feeble hands against the march of a fighting country. Of course, while the country was at war, it was inevitable, he supposed, that they should be dealt with, as they had resisted the will to war. But they should have been given a few months, as they would have been in England.

He had sustained the Espionage Act of 1917, which made it a crime to resist the draft, to preach against the draft, for the words in question had a direct effect on the draft, and were intended to impede it; and when a country was at war even words could be prohibited, words that in ordinary times and places would have been innocent enough and would have been protected by the constitutional guaranty of freedom of speech. He was aware that the Chief Justice had picked him to voice their unanimous decision, the Chief knowing well his instinct for freedom of speech, a freedom bred in his very bone and blood. Below the instinct his brethren little suspected that even if he took the most extreme view in favor of free speech, on the plane of the abstract, he had no very enthusiastic belief in its effectiveness—though he hoped he would die for it. But war was war, the circumstances changed, not the principle.

The case involved the usual drivel of the ignorant and uneducated. "Assert . . . your rights . . . cunning politicians . . . a mercenary capitalist press . . . the rights of the people. . ." He had sustained the right of his nation at war to punish such talk. That was inevitable. But he had tried to formulate a standard. "The question in every case," he wrote in this first test case sustaining the act, *Schenck* v. *United States*, "is whether the words used are used in such circumstances and are of such a nature as to create a clear and present danger that they will bring about the substantive evils that Congress has a right to prevent." He felt the impact of the phrase, and, with an instinct against the closed door of too precise definition, added: "It is a question of proximity and degree."

When a nation is at war many things that might be said in time of peace are such a hindrance to its effort that their utterance will not be endured so long as men fight and that no Court could regard them as protected by any constitutional right.

He knew that men would always fight; and that in battle the will to fight, the very basis of law and of national existence, could not be opposed. But the opposition must lead to clear and present danger, before he would sanction its suppression, even in war.

The phrase has become famous, has been quoted constantly, is today a sort of liberal rudder to hold some direction of objective standard. Its implication has been endlessly discussed; and issues will rise again for further analysis of the authority of its formula. It is improbable that Holmes, who so greatly distrusted phrases and their use to displace the freer play of imaginative thinking, would have been much impressed by such a test as more than an instinctive guide, hardly accurate to chart proximity and degree. But surely it might serve, if not to define a legal principle, at least to suggest a standard of approach, cautious and realistic.

Schenck had been sentenced to six months. Frohwerk got ten years for distributing similar literature to obstruct the draft, soon after we had declared war against Germany, and Holmes was again chosen to write the opinion sustaining the conviction. Again it seemed to him a petty business for the nation to pick up and prosecute; but their decision, on appeal, could not be different. Free speech was no absolute right; the whole conception of absolute rights was alien to the balanced necessity of human society. A man may not falsely shout fire in a theatre and cause a panic, he had said in the *Schenck* case; and added here that no competent person ever supposed that to make criminal the counselling of murder would be an unconstitutional interference with free speech. As usual in any case for nice decision the two opposing principles—here freedom of speech and the waging of war—expanded till the circles touched, and the tangent was exactly where you had to draw the line. There had been no special effort to reach men subject to the draft, and the penalty had been very severe for the utterances of the usual ignorant commonplaces about a war of Wall Street to save rich men's sons. But it might be found that "the circulation of the paper was in quarters where a little breath would be enough to kindle a flame. . ." He felt a distaste for the whole business, including his inevitable part in it, the lack of proportion in the whole thing.

But if the decision was distasteful it was not hard. It seemed to him obvious that words having as their natural tendency and reasonable effect to obstruct recruiting service could be made punishable in war-time; and he said so again in the third case under the Espionage Act, involving Eugene Debs, who had been sentenced to ten years for saying that all war, and that this war in particular, was inspired by capitalism, and that the master class declared wars which the subject class fought, and so on, the usual discourse. In writing the three opinions he detailed at length what the defendants urged, unlike his usual practice which was to plunge into the heart of the issue with hardly more than a reference to the facts which supported it. The talk, thus spread out, seemed shabby enough, almost innocent in its pattern of mild cant phrases—but enough to support conviction. Whether it was enough to justify putting into motion the complicated wheels of government machinery, ah! that was a different question, but a question which his New England conscience, his sense of sane human justice, could not shrug away.

A year later came the *Abrams* case, and Holmes' famous dissent. It is obvious that he is moved by a deep sense of outrage, a feeling of shame that the surreptitious publishing of this silly leaflet by an unknown man, without more, should have been punished by twenty years in prison! The majority used language which seemed to him to have no application to what actually had been done, tall talk almost as futile and inappropriate as the condemned language before them, out of which the majority was able to invoke a plan to excite "disaffection, sedition, riots, and . . . revolution, in this country for the purpose of embarrassing and if possible defeating the military plans of the Government in Europe."

American troops had been sent to Russia in 1917, after the revolution, and a few Russians met in the basement room of a shabby house in New York. They printed a few thousand leaflets of protest, scattered them from the roof, distributed them secretly. Four men and a girl were caught. Three were sentenced to twenty years each, one fifteen years, and one three years. One leaflet spoke of the President's cowardly silence about the intervention in Russia, the hypocrisy of the plutocratic gang in Washington, the "German militarism combined with allied capitalism to crush the Russian revolution." It ended, with the usual: "Awake! Awake, you Workers of the World! Revolutionists." The

other leaflet exhorted the Russian emigrants to spit
in the face of false military propaganda; said the
money they had lent would "make bullets not only
for the Germans but also for the Workers Soviets
of Russia . . . to murder not only the Germans,
but also your dearest, best, who are in Russia and
are fighting for freedom." The leaflet ended by
suggesting that the reply to this "barbaric intervention" be a general strike. "Woe unto those who
will be in the way of progress. Let solidarity live!
The Rebels."

Of course, said Holmes, these pronunciamentos
did urge the curtailment of production for the
prosecution of the war within the meaning of the
statute. But the statute required an "intent . . . to
cripple or hinder the United States in the prosecution of the war;" and he could not find that the
intent had been proved; that is, the intent in the
strict and accurate sense in which he believed it was
used—the aim or purpose to produce the conse-
quence.

But the more important aspect of the case, he
thought, was the First Amendment, forbidding the
Congress to abridge freedom of speech. In the
Schenck and *Frohwerk* and *Debs* cases he had rec-

ognized that speech could be punished that produced clear and imminent danger; doubtless more
readily in time of war. But even in war the principle is the same—the present danger of immediate
evil. He could find no such danger to the Government.

Deeply he felt the profound injustice of the long
sentences. He was disturbed that his country could
have done publicly anything so ignoble.

In this case, [he wrote] sentences of twenty years
imprisonment have been imposed for the publishing of
two leaflets that I believe the defendants had as much
right to publish as the Government has to publish the
Constitution of the United States now vainly invoked
by them. Even if I am technically wrong and enough
can be squeezed from these poor and puny anonym-
ities to turn the color of legal litmus paper . . . the
most nominal punishment seems to me all that pos-
sibly could be inflicted, unless the defendants are to
be made to suffer not for what the indictment alleges
but for the creed that they avow—a creed that I
believe to be the creed of ignorance and immaturity
when honestly held. . .

Writing these words he felt his inadequacy to
make them burn with the resentment and passionate
conviction that he felt. The issue far transcended

these three poor men, so unimportant, and the girl, the victims of the hysteria of a war that had now been fought. It touched and tested the very experiment of life on which the American way, for which he had fought, and which he loved, was founded. He wrote:

But when men have realized that time has upset many fighting faiths, they may come to believe even more than they believe the very foundations of their own conduct that the ultimate good desired is better reached by free trade in ideas—that the best test of truth is the power of the thought to get itself accepted in the competition of the market, and that truth is the only ground upon which their wishes safely can be carried out. That at any rate is the theory of our Constitution. It is an experiment, as all life is an experiment. Every year if not every day we have to wager our salvation upon some prophecy based upon imperfect knowledge. While that experiment is part of our system I think that we should be eternally vigilant against attempts to check the expression of opinions that we loathe and believe to be fraught with death, unless they so imminently threaten immediate interference with the lawful and pressing purposes of the law that an immediate check is required to save the country.

He sent a copy of the opinion to Pollock, who

was surprised with the sentence. In England a few months would have been thought adequate.

I do not think the great dissent added anything to the "clear and present danger" test suggested in the *Schenck* case; nor indeed stated a constitutional view which later became the law, as with so many of Holmes' dissenting opinions. The point where expression of opinion becomes incitement cannot be tested only by the possibility of its success. But the splendid language of the great dissent may make it impossible, or at least difficult, for the clash of this new war to produce another *Abrams* case. And the dissent, if it has not made law, has added to our national heritage a concept of freedom to speak that Americans will cherish as long as they cherish that freedom.

Benjamin Gitlow was convicted, a few years later, under a New York State statute for writing *The Left Wing Manifesto*, that advocated the Communist revolution, the class struggle, revolutionary mass action, and the dictatorship of the proletariat. The Supreme Court refused to hold that the statute unconstitutionally deprived Gitlow of his freedom of expression. The language, said the Court, was not mere abstract expression, but was direct incitement. Holmes, dissenting (with Brandeis), found the phrase unsatisfactory as a test. "Every idea," he said, "is an incitement. . . The only difference between the expression of an opinion and an incitement in the narrower sense is the speaker's enthusiasm for the result. Eloquence may set fire to reason. But whatever may be thought of the redundant discourse before us it had no chance of starting a present conflagration." In a letter to Pollock he spoke of his dissent "in favor of the rights of an anarchist (so-called) to talk drool in favor of the proletarian dictatorship. But the prevailing notion of free speech seems to be that you may say what you choose if you don't shock *me*."

Ten years after the war the intolerance that had been bred by the war had not disappeared. Rosika Schwimmer, an avowed pacifist, was denied citizenship because she said that in a war she would not bear arms, and was for that reason deemed not to be attached to the principles of the Constitution. Holmes dissented, with quiet irony. "So far as the adequacy of her oath is concerned I hardly can see how that is affected by the statement [of her views], inasmuch as she is a woman over fifty years of age, and would not be allowed to bear arms if she wanted to." She believed in organized government, and held "none of the now-dreaded creeds. . . Surely it cannot show lack of attachment to the principles of the Constitution that she thinks that it can be improved." He did not share her optimism that war would disappear "and that the impending destiny of mankind is to unite in peaceful leagues." Yet her optimistic anticipations hardly showed that she would make a bad citizen.

Some of her answers might excite popular prejudice, but if there is any principle of the Constitution that more imperatively calls for attachment than any other it is the principle of free thought—not free thought for those who agree with us but freedom for the thought that we hate. . . The Quakers have done their share to make the country what it is . . . and . . . I had not supposed hitherto that we regretted our inability to expel them because they believe more than some of us do in the teachings of the Sermon on the Mount.

The opinion was designed, he told Owen Wister, to occasion discomfort in certain quarters.

XI

HE WAS eighty years old. Sir Frederick and Lady Pollock had cabled congratulations, and Holmes at once sat down to let them know that it would have been a good deal harder to turn the corner of eighty if they had not been there. The newspapers and periodicals, particularly the few liberal ones, and the law reviews had been gratifyingly eloquent, as if, it occurred to him, his age had made them forget that he was more brilliant than sound. . .

He was tired, and Fanny made him take a nap in the afternoon. That suppressed excitement of hers was hardly accounted for by the fact that they were to dine out at a "pot house," not because it was his birthday, which did not come for two days, but because it was Sunday night, and they had been dining out on Sunday night for fifty years. It was more fun to go to the New Willard than it had been at the Parker House. Fanny had insisted that he dress, tails and all. She was unaccountably slow, and wouldn't let him go downstairs till she was ready. He was hungry and restless. What *was* she up to?

The secretaries must have come up through the kitchen, for when the folding doors slid open, there they were, standing around the dinner table; and he shaded his eyes, as he looked at them. "Ghosts! . . . Well I'll be damned. . ." And there was enough champagne, left over from the days before that moral tornado had swept the country. There were, in fact, three untasted bottles that Henry White had sent him, not so long ago, that had perplexed his conscience. And he had said to himself, and later to others, more than once: "The Eighteenth Amendment forbids manufacture, transportation and importation. It does not forbid possession or use. If I send it back I shall be guilty of transportation. On the whole I think I shall apply the maxim *de minimis*, and drink it. . ." The talk had sounded good, and he had smoked one extra cigar, while his boys smoked interminable cigarettes.

Among the mass of birthday letters was one from J. C. H. Wu, a young Chinese student at the Michigan Law School. There was an eager admiration, and a note of youthful, generous ambition, that

appealed to the older man, and troubled him a little.
He must write the boy a few lines, that could not
help being a little stiff, as he had never seen him.
They sounded like those of every father to every
son. "I hope," he warned, "you will not shirk the
details and drudgery that life offers, but will master
them as the first step to bigger things." He thought
how he himself had not shirked the drudgery, fifty
years ago, carrying his precious notes everywhere
he went in the green bag, refusing to let the spring
or the Cosmos tempt his steps from the path. The
boy sounded a little highfalutin—but he remembered what he had been like at that age, and sent
for the *Michigan Law Review* in which Wu
had said was his article, "Reading from Ancient
Chinese Codes and Other Sources of Chinese Law
and Legal Ideas." He had been mistaken—here was
no beginner, but apparently a ripe scholar. Holmes
at once wrote an apology for his former tone. He
suggested that these liberal translations giving the
spirit of the texts were refinements that didn't realize the cruder reality—"inarticulate dictate of nature" sounded subtler than Lao-tzŭ. Holmes had
once referred to the Gilbert Murray translations of
Euripides as "Swinburne and Water." Like his

great-great-grandmother, Temperance Hewet, he preferred to struggle through the original Greek with a dictionary.

There are some fifty letters to Wu covering the next ten years. Wu's letters to the Justice have not been published; but from the beginning they must have been filled with an unrestrained personal admiration that occasionally embarrassed the New Englander, with his dislike of the superlative, but that also pleased him and tempted him into a more personal expression than usual. He felt uncomfortable when Wu called him a "hero." Of course he'd done his job respectably in the war, but he was not born for soldiering, for the endless planning of details that made a successful soldier; he hadn't accomplished anything particularly remarkable. There were also certain characteristics unfolding from Wu's letters that worried him a bit, as he began to take more interest in the young man—his naïve assumption that war would cease if men would only act reasonably, for instance. Reason was not what controlled men, but their desires, and to attain these they would always fight. Wu had a way of using long philosophers' words, which made you suspect that perhaps he did not have the inborn gift of insight. "The great thing," Holmes wrote him, "is to have an eye for the essential. If a boy gets his fingers pinched between two inward revolving wheels, it probably will only distract attention and bore the reader to describe the machinery." If all experience is art, as Croce says, art is caricature in the sense that the artist drops all else except what he intends to make you feel.

Wu's raptures, too, disquieted him a bit, either when Wu was writing about Holmes or talking about the law, for Holmes was afraid the raptures would be dimmed when Wu got into the actualities. How worried he himself had been, at Wu's age, that the law, on which he had bet his life, would disappoint him. But it had not. He felt a yearning of protective instinct to the lad, who somehow didn't sound tough, as he himself had been tough. Wu seemed to attribute some mystic entity to the law, when, for instance, he asked if it was a monad. Holmes hinted at this fear; but added that he hoped "you bear the fire in your belly"—a nice message from an old fellow to a young Chinese boy.

Wu wrote an article for the *Michigan Law Review*, "The Juristic Philosophy of Justice Holmes," and sent him the notes in advance. Wu had laid it

on a little too thick. "I should prefer," Holmes
wrote back, "to be as little as may be a party to
praises of myself;" and he had presently to reiterate:
"As I said, I should like to have as little as possible
to do with publishing praises of myself. I do not
wish to seem to be conspiring to get my horn
blown. . ."

He was afraid Wu's taste for philosophy might
lead him too far from the concrete. He should nour-
ish his abstractions with the particulars that give
them value. One must see the universal in the particular, but any particular was as good as another.
One could know and therefore believe nothing
about absolute truth. One must begin with an act
of faith, deciding that one is not God, and then
one is not dreaming the world. And one can speculate about it. But one cannot *prove* one is awake.
"I regard myself," he wrote, "as a cosmic ganglion
—a part of an unimaginable and don't venture to
assume that my *can't helps* which I call reason and
truth are cosmic *can't helps*." So Wu's assumption
that this is the best possible world struck Holmes
as an assumption *in vacuo*, "churning the void to
make cheese." "I do not know," he confesses,
"whether our ultimates such as good and bad, ideals,

for the matter of that, consciousness, are cosmic ultimates or not. They seem to me to bear marks of the human and the finite."

Wu suggested that he give a year to Spinoza. The wisdom of this relaxation from sordid and uninteresting details raised a doubt in his friend's mind—that is, if Wu was to study law. The view of this life and this world was more manifold, more exquisite, more profound than anything that could be got out of the past. A horse must eat hay as well as oats. It is better to study the practical aspects of the law and show your power in transfiguring its details than to attempt to see it *sub specie aeternitatis.* He had tried to put his feeling of the infinite into law, to exhibit the detail with whatever hint of vista he could. It was better to do that up to the end than to write an autobiography. . . And another thought, Wu, which occurs to me: Forms are useful only to present their contents, "just as the only use of a pint pot is to present the beer (or whatever lawful liquid it may contain), and infinite meditation upon the pot never will give you the beer. . ." He wondered if the Oriental mind meditated perhaps endlessly on form. He wondered about Wu. Was he reaching for a form that was not his own?

Was he yielding to the convenience of the technical language of philosophy, like those cursed Germans?

Wu wrote he was coming to Washington; and the old gentleman had himself driven to the *Cosmos Club*, where he had heard the food was pretty decent. He reserved a room at $1.25 a day, as he knew Wu couldn't afford much. The club seemed a bit stuffy, full of professors and fellows who looked as if they were economists. But he guessed Wu wouldn't mind, and the young fellow mustn't squander his money. He wrote Wu, in that delicate, meticulous hand: "I told the Cosmos Club to reserve a room for you on Dec. 20. It costs $1.25 which is very cheap for these parts. I did not have time to inspect it but they assured me that it was a good room like others occupied by members of the Club including McChord of the Inter-State Commerce Commission except that it is not a corner room. I understood that a bath room and so forth are near at hand. . . Also tell me what hour you arrive." He was excited to see the lad. His heart warmed to think how much they would exchange. He hoped Wu would not be disappointed. And when they had met, and spent two or three delight-

ful evenings together, his affection for Wu was
genuine and conscious; but he wasn't sure, in spite
of the scholarship and maturity, that Wu had the
fire in his belly.

He worried about Wu when for long periods of
time he did not hear from him. Wu was back in
China, teaching law, and things were pretty bad
there, especially for a young liberal. He was worried even more about Wu's strength of independence. Wu had asked him for a small loan, which
he had refused; or at least had not answered the
letter. Wu ought not to ask him for money. He had
never asked any one for money. Wu should stand
on his own feet, and not speculate too much about
what he called this miserable world. The world was
always miserable until you made it yours. But of
course he knew that lonely ebbing of faith, he had
been through those doubts of the value of the whole
show. . . But to live was not to doubt.

He sat down and wrote a long letter to Wu, and
told him about his reading—the little reading that
an old man could manage, not as strong as he once
was, who had had an old man's operation a year or
two ago, so that he could no longer run up the stairs
two steps at a time, but had to crawl up with the

elevator they had put in for him; the reading snatched from those precious moments of leisure, when the last opinion was out of his system, all his letters written: Seneca, rather long-winded moralizing, some of Plutarch's *Essays* (but in the translation), Plautus, rudimentary humors like the circus, two books of Tacitus, Santayana's *Scepticism and Animal Faith*, the theme almost lost in variations and arabesques, with that Catholic air of ironic superiority. It is the modern books, not the classics, however, that give the latest and most profound conceptions. The literature of the past is a bore (subject of course to such private exceptions as one would make). It does not have our emphasis, or ask or answer our questions.

He was afraid he might not be able to help Wu in his plans to found an institution of law. He hoped that his own uselessness would not "check the generous ardor of your soul." He would pass eighty-five in a few months, and the papers spoke of him as the Venerable Justice, though his feelings still had some of the illusions of youth. When he had a case to write he was all there, but then he was often inclined to lie down and often to sleep, and had become a little slack about improving his mind in the interests of his work. . . He had begun to sign himself "affectionately" to Wu.

Would Wu understand his philosophy? It was important that he should, for Wu must not reflect the theological attitude. He wrote to Wu his own belief "that we are in the universe, not it in us. . . we are part of an unimaginable, which I will call a whole, in order to name it." Because the cosmos may produce intelligence out of the course of its energy there is no reason to suppose that for me this marks any ultimate. "I suspect that all my ultimates have the mark of the finite upon them, but as they are the best I know I give them practical respect. . . We must be serious in order to get work done, but when the usual Saturday half holiday comes I see no reason why we should not smile at the trick by which nature keeps us at our job." It is encouraging to believe that one has done something that one would have liked to do. "But in the subterranean misgivings I think, I believe that I think sincerely, that it does not matter much." He felt curiously close to Wu now that, a bit shyly, he had given to him something of his inner convictions. . .

Wu wrote an appendix for a translation of Stammler's *Theory of Justice*, and sent the book to

Holmes. Wu's admiration for Stammler worried Holmes. The book elaborated the obvious in scholastic language, reflecting the German method of over-systematizing. "How I hate to say anything discouraging to you," he wrote Wu, "but I do not perceive in what you have written anything likely to influence profoundly, as you expect, the development of legal science." He at least must make Wu see where he stood. There were no *a priori* ultimates—not even that man is an end in himself. "We march up a conscript with bayonets behind to die for a cause he doesn't believe in. And I feel no scruples about it. Our morality seems to me only a check on the ultimate domination of force, just as our politeness is a check on the impulse of every pig to put his feet in the trough." "Legal science" was the wrong approach—the existing notions of public policy were the only principles worth talking about. What good to put a new ticket on the well-known process that decisions followed earlier decisions that were not identical on the ground that the policy implied covered the present case? He hated to discourage Wu. He would send Wu's paper to Pound, who might see more in it.

Wu had been made a judge of the Shanghai Provisional Court, and Holmes was glad because Wu would now see how the law takes hold of people in life, instead of continuing to speculate without the necessary raw material. . . Soon Holmes would be eighty-six, and felt some of the self-distrust of age, but not enough to discourage him from keeping on; and he wrote to Wu, he hoped not enough to make Wu feel that he might change toward his old friend. . . He advised Wu about his opinions —don't be too free with theoretical views. He hoped Wu would not try to come here to lecture. Wu was beginning to run the long race, was getting life by the throat, was putting his neck into the collar. He should live in China and make himself felt there instead of wasting precious energy in restlessness and curvetting about.

It was the spring of 1928. Holmes was eighty-seven. He had been reading Parrington's *Main Currents of American Thought*—interesting except that it displeased him "from a sort of dogmatic implication of the obvious connection of views that I don't share." He hated the drivelling cant about " 'exploitation' as a hostile characterization of modern commercial life," implying that "dominant brains are to blame. . . Well, my dear boy, I could ramble on if you were here, but this is enough for writing, especially as there are those who say that my Ms. is hard to read. I tell my brethren when they complain that they ought to go to a night school. . ." There were some cases in the last term that "seemed to have some wiggle of life in them. . ." He was reading Bertrand Russell's *Philosophy*, whose general view of the universe seemed to wobble between sentiment and reason. . . He had heard from Laski that Wu was building a reputation in China. He hoped he wouldn't press his idea of coming to Harvard for a year—it would defeat his opening campaign. "It seems at this distance," he wrote, "as if when the first time came to face the disagreeable, to eat food that seems to have little nourishment in it and in short to tackle the unromantic in life with resolution to make it romantic, you were not willing and able to do this heroic thing."

He adds: "I have idled in the sun, walked a very little and motored a good deal and slept. Things seem to be going well with me and if I live to October 4 or 5 I shall be older than Taney was when he died and I rather think the oldest judge who has been on the bench at my age, a silly little matter for which of course I do not really care."

When Wu finally decided to go to Harvard, Holmes sent Pound a check to help make up the scholarship fund. There was no need to say anything about it to Wu.

Wu sent Holmes his book *Juridical Essays and Studies* in the autumn of 1928; and, in thanking him, the old man, who was depressed from a cold that had kept him in the house, could not help thinking of his chances of ever seeing Wu again, for now he was "the oldest judge who ever has remained sitting on our Bench," and for a month had lived even longer than Taney. He felt his inadequacies, and had a dreadful doubt whether the three Chinese lads who had called the other day had got what they wanted. But no one can direct the life of another man. He understood Wu's inner want of self-confidence, for he had suffered the black years, but had had luck. . . To sum it all there must be faith in effort, before you can see the goal or put articulately the question to be asked. It is the force of will, the capacity to want something fiercely, to stick to the rugged course. . .

XII

OWEN WISTER had sent him two books of this new American writer, Ernest Hemingway, *Men Without Women* and *The Sun Also Rises*, which, as Holmes wrote Pollock, Wister seemed to think of great promise when the writer got away from his garbage. He reported to Wister on *The Sun Also Rises*.

We both agree with you that there is something quite remarkable about the author, although my wife backed out when it came to the bull fights, which she didn't want to read out, and she had had enough. It is singular. An account of eating and drinking with a lot of fornication accompanied by conversations on the lowest level, with some slight intelligence but no ideas, and nothing else—and yet it seems a slice of life, and you are not bored with details of an ordinary day.

It reminds me of a reflection that I often make on how large a part of the time and thoughts of even the best of us are taken up by animal wants. These lads so far as appears don't think of anything else. And I sometimes say that if a man contributes neither thought nor beauty to life—as is the case with the majority—I would let Malthus loose on him. But then this lad could write this book, which must be a work of art. It can't be accident and naïveté. So let him survive—but as you prophesied that he would, let him leave his garbage.

He added that he had done some law in anticipation of the next term, was reading Morison's *Oxford History of the United States* and generally improving his mind so far as was consistent with good drives and long snoozes in the daytime. But to Pollock, six weeks later, he wrote: "I am trying to feel unscrupulous and to read . . . for amusement but it comes very hard."

Wister protested that "thought and beauty" was too exclusive; and Holmes was quick to correct the impression.

You could not think [he wrote] that I meant by the too narrow words that I used . . . to exclude the glorious company that you name (By the by I do not remember Lady Glencora—who and where is she —I ask blushing not to know). My general thesis is addressed, really, to the common talk of manual labor. It says I built the house—I should have the whole value of it. To which I reply all that man contributes is the *direction* of energy. He does not create his

forces, which can be got cheaper from the stream or
the lightning. His contribution is simply to determine
how it shall be applied. The bricklayer sees that the
brick shall be laid level (unless machinery puts the
need of direction further back). But the architect
determines and contributes much more. And after his
thought has been distributed by the retail dealers,
professors, parsons, essayists, Descartes or Kant, perhaps after a hundred years, governs action on a still
larger scale. I suspect that labor always has hated the
fable of the belly and the members. All of which does
not touch art—the other necessary of life. In opinions
occasionally I have given a light touch to our not
recognizing as necessary anything but the satisfaction
of animal needs.

He had found Morison admirable and just, with
a rare occasional hint of a prejudice he didn't share,
"and once in a while a rather pert flip at the end of
a sentence. He made me reconsider prejudices of
my own." He had been reading Wyndham Lewis'
book on Villon, "written with a sort of Catholic
swagger that makes one wonder whether the author
is as devout as he talks, and padded, but full of interest and instruction." But a bag of *certiorari* had
just come in, and letters from people swelling with
a sense of their wrong and vaguely urging him to
set things right. "So it is not all gaiety."

In December of the same year he was writing Pollock that the carnal man was still strong within him and that he took a good deal of interest in the job—the job of life.

Mrs. Holmes had fallen and broken her hip bone, and for months suffered a good deal of pain, until she died on April 30, 1929. The Justice wrote Pollock: "For sixty years she made life poetry for me and at 88 one must be ready for the end. I shall keep at work and interested while it lasts—though not caring very much for how long." He felt helpless and lonely. Wister proposed himself for a Sunday lunch, and Holmes answered that it would give him pleasure if he would come, "and share my solitary chicken and rather poor home made ice cream. . . I have thought of you many times in these days." Wister wrote to tell him that he enjoyed the lunch, and was planning to sail for Europe, God willing.

You give me so much pleasure [Holmes answered] by saying that you are not sure of sailing till you're off, that I must write a line to say *me too*.

D. V. is a reservation of human vanity so that when destiny plays some trick one can say "Lŏh, I thought of that." But your feeling I suppose is like mine—an apprehension of unanticipated disaster, not a smarty desire to be up with fate.

He felt lost without Fanny to arrange the passage from Washington to Beverly, and wrote Wister that he saw innumerable troubles, even though the trunks had gone after a day's fidget.

A few weeks later, writing from Beverly Farms to Wu, he said:

You may have heard before this of the death of my wife, which not only takes away a half of my life but gives me notice. She was of the same age as I and at 88 the end is due. I may work on for a year or two, but I cannot hope to add much to what I have done. I am too sceptical to think that it matters much, but too conscious of the mystery of the universe to say that it or anything else does not. I bow my head, I think serenely, and say as I told some one the other day, O Cosmos—Now lettest thou thy ganglion dissolve in peace.

He received a letter from Carolyn Kellogg Cushing, whom he had known, nearly seventy years ago, at her mother's house, when he was recruiting a company for the Twentieth Massachusetts. He was moved to hear from her, and wrote:

It is a delight to get your letter, and to realize that you are unchanged from the adorable child of 9. At times I feel finished and often feel sad. A letter like yours revives one's energies. You have the ardor of life, and you pass it on.

He was eighty-nine. His full-length portrait was painted for the Harvard Law School by Charles Hopkinson, and hung in the students' reading room next to the portrait of Marshall. Bishop Lawrence presented the portrait. He was a few years younger than Holmes. "I watched his record," he said, "for we boys were alert to the heroes of those days, and as he was brought back wounded again and again—at Ball's Bluff shot in the breast, at Antietam with a ball in the neck, at Fredericksburg wounded in the foot—he was seen on the streets in Boston, a handsome invalid, to the great delectation of the girls of the city. He was a romantic hero, built for it."

The portrait pleased him and the honor that it was hung as a pendant to Marshall. He wrote to the Law School that this marked the culmination of his life and left him ready to say: "Now lettest thou thy servant depart in peace."

In a month he would be ninety. Wister wrote him he was coming down to Washington to see him. The thought cheered him and he wrote his friend, "dear Whisker," that he was to sit for a bust by a Russian sculptor, "well-spoken of, Sergei Konenkov, with a good looking wife who does the talking and keeps the sitter entertained." He added, a little ruefully, that the promised leisure—it keeps recurring through all his letters with the wistful glow of the unattainable—was mostly vanishing. He quoted:

> I never had a piece of bread
> Particularly long and wide
> But fell upon the sanded floor,
> And always on the buttered side.

"My sec. has read to me the Newcomes," he continued. "Thackeray, I suspect, got part of his pleasantness from Addison and Steele, but owes much to the half hidden music of his style. A little too much gravy for the holiness of a good woman and Sunday worship—but perhaps the time required it. We will jaw anon—unless I have a previous engagement at Arlington which I do not anticipate."

He was ninety years old! It was an incredible fact, and he was rather proud of it. Frankfurter had

collected a number of articles about him that had
appeared during the last fifteen years, written by
Morris R. Cohen, John Dewey, Frankfurter,
Learned Hand, Harold J. Laski, Walter Lippmann,
Philip Littell, Josef Redlich, Elizabeth Shepley
Sergeant, John H. Wigmore, with an introduction
by Benjamin N. Cardozo, and had put them in a
book "as symbols of our homage and affection."
Pollock had cabled Holmes that he had been elected
an Honorary Bencher of Lincoln's Inn, the first
time that they had "gone outside the four seas," as
Pollock was pleased to put it. Pollock had also cele-
brated the event in the *Columbia Law Review*, and
all day the letters and telegrams had poured in. In
the *Yale Law Journal* there were articles by Harold
J. Laski and Hessel E. Yntema; in the *Harvard Law
Review* the Lord Chancellor and the Attorney
General of Great Britain joined Pollock, Cardozo,
Chief Justice Hughes, Roscoe Pound, then Dean of
the Harvard Law School, Professors Plucknett and
Frankfurter in tributes. The *Harvard Graduates'
Magazine* hailed him as "the most distinguished
Harvard graduate now in public life." Robert
Marshall, exploring in Alaska, had found an undis-
covered mountain and named it after Holmes to

commemorate his birthday; and the old gentleman was pleased, and wrote Marshall's brother-in-law, Jacob Billikopf, that he was proud of this indication of Marshall's regard for him, adding: "For we don't get rid of interest in ourselves even when Self is so near vanishing."

The day before his ninetieth birthday he had been to the usual Saturday conference of the Court. The night of his birthday he was to speak on the radio from his library, and there were to be tributes from the Chief Justice, the Dean of the Yale Law School, the President of the American Bar Association. As he wrote to Dean Clark, who was in charge of the program, he expected to say a few words, "mostly short ones." He had never spoken on the air before, Fanny hadn't approved; she probably wouldn't approve now if she were here, but he thought it would be fun. They were putting on a good show. He liked a good show, he thought, chuckling, liked to have the butter spread on thick, and that was all right if you remembered all the time it *was* butter.

He listened to the others before he spoke. The Chief Justice was speaking, in the rich tones he knew so well. "He has abundantly the zest of life," he heard the Chief say, "and his age crowns that eagerness and unflagging interest with the authority of experience and wisdom. . . We bring to Mr. Justice Holmes our tribute of admiration and gratitude. We place upon his brow the laurel crown of the highest distinction. But this will not suffice us or him. We honor him, but, what is more, we love him. We give him to-night the homage of our hearts."

The old man was deeply moved as those who listened to him knew. He paused for a moment, then spoke quietly, rather slowly. "In this symposium my part is only to sit in silence," he said. "To express one's feelings as the end draws near is too intimate a task."

He paused.

But I may mention [he continued] one thought which comes to me as a listener-in. The riders in a race do not stop short when they reach the goal. There is a little finishing canter before coming to a standstill. There is time to hear the kind voice of friends and to say to one's self: "The work is done." But just as one says that, the answer comes: "The race is over, but the work never is done while the power to work remains." The canter that brings you to a standstill need not be only coming to rest. It cannot be while you still live. For to live is to function. That is all there is in living.

He paused again for a moment, and then—

And so I end with a line from a Latin poet who uttered the message more than fifteen hundred years ago: "Death plucks my ears and says, Live—I am coming."

He had a charming letter of congratulation from Countess Eleanor Palffy, whom he had driven out to Fort Stevens, many years before. "It is enchanting to get a letter from you," he promptly answered her.

Doubly enchanting to get *this* letter. When I am free to drive out in an automobile, I frequently go up through the Riverside, and return through George-town, and always think of your coming down the steps to come with me to Fort Stevens. You left such a vivid impression that, so long as it was possible, I always was hoping that you would come again. Great expectations, but circumstances prevented your com-ing. Your letter arrived this morning and it has made the day happy. One doesn't meet enchantresses every day, and old as I am I still can sit up and take notice.

He told her that the President had sent him a mass of newspaper clippings that it would be a task to read. "Such things generally make me reflect that they don't know anything about it, and I sadly meditate on what I don't know and can't do. But once in a while a word from a master really hits me where I live, and I think that now it is time for me to die. But I enjoy life still, and don't wish to hurry the marching orders, although I believe that I am ready for them." He copied out his radio speech for her. "I wish," he ended, "you had told me as much about yourself as I have told you about me, but you say adorable things. I kiss your hands . . ."

The next week his secretaries came to see him, fifteen out of the twenty-six of them. They had lunched together first in a private room at the May-flower Hotel, and had had their share of cocktails, and had swapped stories about the Judge. George L. Harrison, who was then president of the Federal Reserve Bank of New York, spoke for the rest. Would the Justice consent to sit for another portrait by Charles Hopkinson, to be presented by the secretaries to the Supreme Court and hung in the new building? The old gentleman looked at the secretaries, and rubbed his chin. He didn't know how to put it to them. He muttered something about not liking them to fork up. But the secretaries assured him that they could afford it, they were doing pretty well. He liked the idea. Hopkinson's portrait at the Harvard Law School, painted a year before, had style. . .

When they trooped out of the library he let his mind turn back ten years to the surprise dinner that Fanny had so skillfully managed for his eightieth birthday. . . He could see Fanny jiggling the little red devil with the springy arms and legs that hung under the chandelier in his library, and saying, when he had vented his discouragement in pertinent phrases: "Cheer up Wendell, it's going to be worse!" He could hear her voice again after one of those long, dreary, official dinners in the early days, saying: "Washington is a city where dwell many of the first men of the land and the women they married when they were young. . ."

A month after his ninetieth birthday he was writing to Pollock:

The apple trees around the Potomac basin are in full flower today and the place is packed with automobiles. It is a sight to come hundreds of miles to see. Also the magnolias are coming out and generally I wish the sitting of our Court was at the devil. I want to idle and take in the Spring, but it may not be.

In November he wrote his final will. Edward J. Holmes, his nephew, should have all the editions of the works of his two grandfathers, of his father, and of himself; the pastel of his great-grandfather, Jonathan Jackson, by Copley; his grandfather's desk where he had habitually worked when sitting; the chair marked with the name of Tutor Flynt of Harvard College and that of succeeding owners; and, finally, "the red rug with which the front parlor of my house on Eye Street in Washington, D. C. is carpeted." To Edward and his cousins he bequeathed substantial cash legacies. To the Library of Congress went the rest of his library and his engravings, etchings, and lithographs. Harvard, "preferably for the benefit of the Law School," received $25,000; and the Boston Museum of Fine Arts the same amount. His sister-in-law, Mary Wigglesworth, was to have the rocking chair in his library marked "Nathaniel Bowditch," and the silver that had come from his wife. His servants were remembered in gifts that ranged from $500 to $10,000. The residue of his property he gave to the United States of America.

Another year had gone by, almost another year; and he would have liked to pass another birthday on the Court, in harness. But he was very tired. Now and then Wister came down from Philadelphia to lunch with him, and often sent him books. "I suppose," he wrote Wister, "it means the last pages of the book, but I don't adequately believe and realize it. . . People say you wouldn't know what to do without your court work. I think I could keep leisure pretty busy and be happy without responsibility. I find it hard to write and shall shut up. The radio brought here by my secretary is playing Brahms, Phila. Orchestra, so I am in contact with culture." He found it hard to keep his attention fixed on the arguments, and he would grow drowsy as he listened, stooped over his notes, his head nodding. . . He would start up, writing in sudden concentration at his notes to keep awake. . . He hated to quit. He knew that they were trying to save him, that the Chief Justice was assigning him the easier cases. He came to dread the briefs and the records, the *certiorari* which even the Chief could not shield him from, and he would plunge at them, with a fury of determination that broke against his haunting fatigue. He went to his last conference on Saturday, January 10. On Sunday he made up his mind to resign. The next day he wrote his resignation to President Hoover:

MR. PRESIDENT:

In accordance with the provision of the Judicial Code as amended Section 260, Title 28 United States Code 375, I tender my resignation as Justice of the Supreme Court of the United States of America. The condition of my health makes it a duty to break off connections that I cannot leave without deep regret after the affectionate relations of many years and the absorbing interests that have filled my life. But the time has come and I bow to the inevitable. I have nothing but kindness to remember from you and from my brethren. My last word should be one of grateful thanks.

With great respect, your obedient servant,

OLIVER WENDELL HOLMES.

He sat on Monday for the last time, and told his brethren he had resigned. When he got home he found the President's letter. The President wrote: "I know of no American retiring from public service with such a sense of affection and devotion of the whole people."

And there was a letter from his brethren on the Court. He read it slowly, his hand shaking. They wrote him:

DEAR JUSTICE HOLMES:

We can not permit your long association in the work of the Court to end without expressing our keen sense of loss and our warm affection. Your judicial

Supreme Court in 1930, the last picture of Mr. Justice Holmes with the other members of the Court

Standing, left to right: Harlan Fiske Stone, George Sutherland, Pierce Butler, Owen J. Roberts. Seated: James Clark McReynolds, Oliver Wendell Holmes, Chief Justice Charles Evans Hughes, Willis Van Devanter, Louis D. Brandeis

service of over forty-nine years—twenty years in
the Supreme Judicial Court of Massachusetts and
twenty-nine years upon this bench—has a unique
distinction in uninterrupted effectiveness and excep-
tional quality. Your profound learning and philosophic outlook have found expression in opinions
which have become classic, enriching the literature of
the law as well as its substance. With a most conscien-
tious exactness in the performance of every duty, you
have brought to our collaboration in difficult tasks a
personal charm and a freedom and independence of
spirit which have been a constant refreshment. While
we are losing the privilege of daily companionship,
the most precious memories of your unfailing kindli-
ness and generous nature abide with us, and these
memories will ever be one of the choicest traditions
of the Court.

Deeply regretting the necessity for your retirement,
we trust that—relieved of the burden which had become too heavy—you may have a renewal of vigor
and that you may find satisfaction in your abundant
resources of intellectual enjoyment.

Affectionately yours,

Charles E. Hughes
Willis Van Devanter
James C. McReynolds
Louis D. Brandeis
George Sutherland
Pierce Butler
Harlan F. Stone
Owen J. Roberts.

He must answer them at once, and the last filament that connected him with the Court would be cut. He sat down at his desk, his forehead pressed against his left hand, and answered their letter.

My Dear Brethren:

You must let me call you so once more. Your more than kind, your generous, letter touches me to the bottom of my heart. The long and intimate association with men who so command my respect and admiration could not but fix my affection as well. For such little time as may be left for me I shall treasure it as adding gold to the sunset.

Affectionately yours,

O. W. Holmes.

On his ninety-first birthday the Federal Bar Association gave a dinner in Washington in his honor. He could not go but wrote that he could not say farewell to life and to them in formal words.

Life seems to me like a Japanese picture which our imagination does not allow to end with the margin. We aim at the infinite and when our arrow falls to earth it is in flames.

At times, [he continued] the ambitious ends of life have made it seem to me lonely, but it has not been. You have given me the companionship of dear friends who have helped to keep alive the fire in my heart. If I could think that I had sent a spark to those who come after I should be ready to say Goodbye.

He listened to the tributes, including a letter from the President, which were broadcast from the dinner, sitting in his library at home. The Solicitor General read his letter. He felt like a ghost, but withal a cheerful one, knowing that the end was not far away, that he could not live forever. . .

A month later his secretary was reading aloud to him Spengler's *The Decline of the West,*

a learned, original book, written with incredible German arrogance, [he wrote Pollock] and not in all believed by me, but wonderfully suggestive—an odious animal who must be read. . . He has as swelled a head as man can have and live, but the beast has ideas, many of which I don't know enough to criticise. I wish he was dead. On the other side is that dear delightful Wodehouse. . .

He lived for three more years, and died two days before his ninety-fourth birthday. They were quiet days, in Washington and at Beverly. He saw the cherries bloom twice again around the Potomac. He had got to a point at the very end of his life where he could idle without the sense that he was neglecting some duty. He was waiting peacefully for death, and didn't mind therefore, now that his work was over, that so much of his time was spent in sleep, or that his memory slipped and his attention wandered.

Wister came to see him, and told him a story that should have brought a chuckle. But he couldn't follow to the point. "Sorry, Whiskers," he said. Then suddenly sitting up, his deep eyes flashing—"I'm living behind a cloud, Whiskers, I'm sorry. But I can still pull my brains together and call a man a son-of-a-bitch if I have to!"

He was very comfortable. Mary and the rest of the household were devoted to him. The secretaries went driving with him, read aloud, while he dozed or listened or played solitaire. Now that his work was done he thought of it as a piece with the rest, so that whether or not he had occasionally touched the superlative hardly seemed to matter. Man respected himself too much and the universe too little. Nature took care of him, for he no longer desired the victuals the doctors forbade—the meat and the wine. Death was not the same thing to an old man as to a young one. He'd had his whack at life, had shown what he could do. He had come to some understanding with himself. To die a little sooner now was only to lose the bits of pleasure that daily grew dimmer, not to miss the point of being. As a youth he'd often felt a pang of anguish that he might never have his opportunity, might never have scope to realize the spontaneous energy of his soul. But now he was ready for the end. He accepted nature, as he had always accepted her. He was waiting the end, peacefully, not very much caring when it came, now his work was over. He added several codicils to his will. He drove whenever the weather was fine. He was fond of driving out to Mount Vernon in the warm weather to smell the box. Regularly once a week, toward the end, he would go out to touch Fanny's tomb, at Arlington. Before long he would be lying by her side. Her tombstone held but her name and the date of her birth and of her death. His would be the same; except that there would be added:

Captain and Brevet Colonel
20th Mass. Vol. Inf., Civil War

Justice Supreme Court of the United States

Driving back, when he had seen the little flags at Arlington, he would think most often of the war in which he had fought. . . "And only in our dreams the guns peal, and the flag is seen . . ." How ghostly the flutter of the lost flag. . . He felt again the incommunicable experience of war, as he once called it. He could see again, as if it were yesterday, the dark electric outline of those in front against the white smoke of the firing, see their line thin and one by one leaders drop from their horses. He rode again by night at a walk toward the blue line of fire at the dead angle of Spottsylvania, where for twenty-four hours they had fought on the two sides of an earthwork. Once more he heard the spat of the bullets upon the trees, in some unknown wood. The encounter had but one end, the burial truce was short. . .

He would try to remember the verses he had quoted at that Memorial Day service of a graduating class at Harvard, almost forty years ago:

And when the wind in the tree-tops roared,
The soldier asked from the deep dark grave:
    "Did the banner flutter then?"
"Not so, my hero," the wind replied,
"The fight is done, but the banner won,
Thy comrades of old have borne it hence,
    Have borne it in triumph hence!"

Then the soldier spake from the deep dark grave:
  "I am content."

. . .

Then he heareth the lovers laughing pass,
  And the soldier asks once more:
"Are these not the voices of them that love,
  That love—and remember me?"
"Not so, my hero," the lovers say,
"We are those that remember not;
For the spring has come and the earth has smiled,
  And the dead must be forgot."
Then the soldier spake from the deep dark grave:
  "I am content."

Now and then he thought he should be improving his mind, now that he had leisure and no more
certiorari; and he wrote to Pollock: "I can imagine
a book on the law, getting rid of all talk of duties
and rights—beginning with the definition of law
in the lawyer's sense as a statement of the circumstances in which the public force will be brought
to bear upon a man through the Courts, and expounding rights as the hypostasis of a prophecy—
in short, systematizing some of my old chestnuts.
But I don't mean to do it or to bother about anything. . ." For after ninety a man is beyond any
duty to improve his mind. Cardozo sent him a copy

of Aristotle's *Ethics*, which once unwarily he had admitted not having read so he could recite on it. He thought he ought to read it. . . . He managed to get through it, but he admitted to his secretary it almost killed him.

He said to a friend:

I am very well taken care of indeed by my excellent secretary and my excellent housekeeper, who trot along, one on each side of me. If I get off the path a little to the right, my housekeeper bites me on my right ear. If I get off a little to the left, my secretary bites me on my left ear. And so I keep well on the path.

One of the former secretaries, who was working in Washington, often came to see him, especially in the evenings, and would take his turn in reading aloud to the old man. That particular night he had begun Henry Adams' *Mont-Saint-Michel and Chartres*. He read about the *Chanson de Roland*, how it must have been sung after Hastings, for what had happened to Harold at the battle of Hastings had once happened to Roland at Roncesvalles. The old Judge dozed—it was but a few weeks before the end—and now and then looked up to smile. Roland had been left for dead by the Saracens when they fled before the horns of Charlemagne's returning host. "Roland," the young man read, "came back to consciousness on feeling a Saracen marauder tugging at his sword Durendal. With a blow of his ivory horn—*oliphant* —he killed the pagan; then feeling death near, he prepared for it." The young man looked up. The old man sat very straight, his eyes shining with a distant fire. The reader continued: "His first thought was for Durendal, his sword, which he could not leave to infidels. . . Three times he struck with all his force against the rock; each time the sword rebounded without breaking. The third time—" The old man's eyes were very bright, the fingers of his right hand, which age had never robbed of that slim and sensitive elegance, drummed a faint tattoo. He was once again at White Oak Swamp, at Antietam, on the Jerusalem Road. Again for an instant his heart had stopped as he listened for the long roll of fire from the main line. . . And after a moment the old man dozed again.

Justice Holmes died of bronchial pneumonia on March 6, 1935. He had been ill less than a week. Two days later, on what would have been his ninety-fourth birthday, he was buried at the Arlington National Cemetery. A Unitarian service was conducted at All Souls' Church in Washington by the Reverend Ulysses G. B. Pierce, who, after readings from the Scriptures, quoted Holmes' own words: "We accept our destiny to work, to fight, to die for ideal aims. At the grave of a hero who has done these things, we end, not with sorrow at the inevitable loss, but with the contagion of his courage; and with a kind of desperate joy we go back to the fight." The Chief Justice and six Associate Justices of the United States Supreme Court were pallbearers, following the coffin up the aisle, the Chief Justice and Mr. Justice McReynolds walking first, and at the end, walking alone, Mr. Justice Cardozo, who had taken the dead man's place on the Court, his head bowed, a sense of the Nation's sadness and its pride on his sensitive, finely chiseled face. . . The coffin, draped in a flag, was borne to Arlington on a caisson, the muffled drums beating a slow march time. A military band played the *Battle Hymn of the Republic*. The President stood at attention, his head bared. There was a triple volley in salute from the rifles of eight infantrymen. Taps sounded.

"I thought he was immortal," some one said.

INDEX

A

Abrams v. *United States*, 111, 158, 163
Adams, Charles Francis, 23
Adams, Henry, 4, 19, 21, 22, 125, 126, 206
Adams, John, 116
Adams, John Quincy, 19, 103
Agassiz, Louis, 23
Allen, Charles, 104
American Bar Association Journal, 112
American Law Journal, 53
Ames, James Barr, 67
Antietam, 28, 32, 33, 188, 207
Arlington National Cemetery, 203, 208
Asquith, Margot, 4
Atlantic Monthly, 28

B

Barlow, Robert, 147
Bartlett, Sidney, 50, 51
Battle Hymn of the Republic, 208
Beck, James M., 144–147
Beverly, Mass., 137, 187, 201
Biddle, Edmund Randolph, 20, 21
Biddle, Francis, 7, 8, 11, 20
Billikopf, Jacob, 191
Blackstone, 59, 61
Blaine: *Twenty Years in Congress*, 78
Boston, 19, 21, 26, 31, 42, 55, 68, 82, 102, 137, 154, 188; Bar Association of, 98; College Law School, 124; Museum of Fine Arts, 196
Bowditch, Henry P., 47, 48, 137
Bowditch, Nathaniel, 196
Brandeis, Louis D., 52, 82, 87, 152, 164, 199
Brooks, Van Wyck, 21–23
Bryce, James, 4
Buffalo Law School, 11
Bundy, Harvey Hollister, 11
Butler, Pierce, Sr., 55
Butler, Pierce, 65, 199

C

Caird: *Social Philosophy and Religion of Comte*, 13, 14
Calhoun, John, 111
California, Constitution of, 127
Cardozo, Benjamin N., 190, 205, 208
Carlyle, Thomas, 26, 43
Carter, John C., 60
Cather, Willa, 59
Chaliapin, Feodor, 151, 152
Chapman, John Jay, 78
Chicago, 154; Bar Association of, 105
Choate, Joseph H., 103, 122, 123
Civil War, The, 12, 16, 31, 88
Clarke, Stanley, 11
Clay, Henry, 20, 111
Cohen, Morris R., 2, 124, 190
Columbia Law Review, 190

209

INDEX

Common Law, The, 4, 53, 55–58, 62, 67, 86
Consolidated Gas case, 113
Constitution of the United States, 96, 107, 123, 127–130, 161, 162, 164, 165
Contract, 132
Coolidge, Calvin, 60
Corcoran, Thomas, 11
Corwin, Edward S., 121
Cowper, Henry, 41
Cropley, Charles Elmore, 110
Cushing, Carolyn Kellogg, 187

D

Dana, Richard H., 21, 23
Dante, 134, 135
Darwin, Charles, 86
Davis, John W., 123
Debs, Eugene, case of, 158, 160
Denby, Charles, 11
Dewey, John, 190
Dicey, Albert V., 4
Dixwell, Fanny Bowditch, cf. Holmes, Fanny Dixwell
Dragon of Wantley, The, 76

E

Eighteenth Amendment, 168
Eliot, Charles W., 67
Emerson, Ralph Waldo, 4, 21, 23–26, 35–37, 57, 79
Emmons, Frank, 137
England, 72, 74, 86, 91
Espionage Act of 1917, 154, 158
Evarts, William Maxwell, 51

F

Federal Bar Association, 200
Federal Reserve Bank of New York, 194

First Amendment, 160
Fourteenth Amendment, 129
Frank, Jerome, 63
Frankfurter, Felix, 4, 12, 89, 128, 189, 190
Franklin, Benjamin, 15
Frohwerck case, 156, 160
Fuller, Margaret, 21
Fuller, Melville Weston, 108–110, 112, 116, 119

G

Gavit v. *United States,* 144
Gitlow, Benjamin, 163
Gold Clause cases, 65
Grant, Ulysses S., 16
Gray, Horace, 11, 12, 103, 114
Gray, John Chipman, 4, 12, 46–48
Green Bag, The, 106

H

Hagerstown, 28, 32
Haldane, Lord, 3, 4
Hamilton, Alexander, 16
Hammer v. *Dagenhart,* 65, 131
Hand, Learned, 190
Harlan, John Marshall, 107, 108, 111, 114
Harriman, Edward H., 9
Harrison, George L., 11, 194
Harvard, class of 1861, speech on fiftieth anniversary of, 135; class of 1895, speech to graduating, 92; College, 27, 55, 138, 196; Graduates Magazine, 190; Law Review, 190; Law School, 11, 12, 28, 39, 53, 67, 70, 89, 109, 195, 196; Law School, Association of New York, 123, 141; Liberal Club,

INDEX

INDEX

213

INDEX